WHAT

WE FIND

IN THE

DARK

Loss, Hope, and God's Presence in Grief

AUBREY SAMPSON

A NavPress resource published in alliance
with Tyndale House Publishers

NavPress.com

What We Find in the Dark: Loss, Hope, and God's Presence in Grief

A NavPress resource published in alliance with Tyndale House Publishers

The Team:
David Zimmerman, Publisher; Caitlyn Carlson, Senior Editor; Elizabeth Schroll, Copyeditor; Olivia Eldredge, Managing Editor; Eva M. Winters, Designer; Sarah Ocenasek, Proofreading Coordinator

Published in association with Tawny Johnson of Illuminate Literary Agency, an Author Management Company, illuminateliterary.com

ISBN 978-1-64158-312-1

Printed in the United States of America

31 30 29 28 27 26 25
7 6 5 4 3 2 1

When loss and disruption come our way, we need trusted guides to help us wander well through such difficult terrain. Aubrey Sampson is one of those people who thoughtfully pastors us in and through the change with grace, wisdom, and depth. What she uncovers and discovers in *What We Find in the Dark* will forever mark how you understand and handle grief. A very timely and necessary read!

STEVE CARTER, pastor and author of *Grieve, Breathe, Receive*

By inviting us into her own dark night of the soul, Aubrey offers hope and light for the seasons of grief, loss, doubt, and suffering that we all encounter. *What We Find in the Dark* provides language for what is often impossible to articulate. It is vulnerable, transparent, honest, and faith filled—a sacred gift.

CHRISTINE CAINE, founder of A21 and Propel Women

Aubrey has taken us behind doors we normally keep shut, giving us an intimate and raw descent into grief. It is a baptism into the depths of sorrow only to find that God is still there. And with God's presence come comfort and hope, but not the kinds that are cheap or trite. The Savior—weeping, wounded, and risen!—is here. It has been said that God does his best work in the dark: from the chaos before creation to the coldness of the grave before resurrection. So, it seems, does Aubrey. This book is a witness to a love that is stronger than death.

GLENN PACKIAM, lead pastor at Rockharbor Church, author of *The Resilient Pastor*, and coauthor of *The Intentional Year*

Aubrey Sampson's words are a loyal companion to anyone who either is in grief or must revisit grief. There is wisdom here that was hard won through real pain. If you are in a season where shallow advice and inspirational quotes are no longer cutting it, you will find this book a welcome salve to your soul. It is for those who need the words to name their tears and the hope of God's nearness in the dark.

FAITH EURY CHO, author of *Experiencing Friendship with God*

With heartfelt honesty, Aubrey Sampson offers palpable comfort to aching hearts overwhelmed by grief and sacred companionship for lonely sojourners navigating the obscurity of the dark. *What We Find in the Dark* radiates glimmers of hope, inviting us to seek, find, and be held by God in our darkest moments.

NATASHA SMITH, author of *Can You Just Sit with Me?*

Aubrey has already taught us how to grieve with God in her seminal work, *The Louder Song*. Now she shows us how to walk faithfully when God seems distant and unresponsive in our pain. From lament to steadfast resolve, Aubrey is not only a fellow traveler but also an experienced guide who will help you uncover God's unique plan for you in the middle of your dark night.

DAVEY BLACKBURN, author of *Nothing Is Wasted*, writer of the Pain to Purpose curriculum, cohost of *The Nothing Is Wasted Podcast*, and founder of Nothing Is Wasted Ministries

Friend, if you are drowning in the darkness of grief, you do not have to walk alone. Aubrey has been to the depths of hopelessness, and she will walk slowly with you through this valley. In these pages you will not feel pressured or pushed, but you may discover a God who sees you even in the dark and a story that can guide your search to solid ground.

CATHERINE McNIEL, coauthor of *Mid-Faith Crisis*

Profoundly raw, deeply personal, beautifully pastoral, and theologically robust—*What We Find in the Dark* is a true gift to those navigating life's shadowed seasons. Aubrey Sampson writes with a poetic grace that meets us in our brokenness and gently guides us toward the God who sees in the dark. Through powerful liturgies, moving stories, and theological depth, she reminds us that even in our deepest losses, we are not abandoned. This book is a faithful companion for anyone seeking hope and comfort in times of grief and spiritual obscurity.

TARA BETH LEACH, pastor and author of *Emboldened*

To the Squad: Kathy, Hollie, and Amanda,

for what we have lost (and also found).

To Kevin, Eli, Lincoln, and Nolan,

for being my flashlights in the dark night.

To my mom: I didn't know we'd need these

words for such a time as this.

I am so sorry we do. I love you so much.

Contents

AN OPENING CONFESSION

THIS IS NOT WHAT I PLANNED FOR

This is not the book I set out to write.

At the beginning, I thought it'd be something like *When You Think Your Life Will Go One Way but It Goes Another (Totally Opposite) Direction.* The writing process was going to be straightforward: researching and typing, mining my life experience, unearthing wisdom from experts, examining the Bible's words on the topic. And, of course, I'd look into an inevitable follow-up question or two: *When our dreams die, how do we live with the gut-wrenching disappointment?* And *Where is God in it all?*

The early threads of that book are still woven into these chapters. The fingerprints of the Aubrey who set out so assuredly to write it are still pressed indelibly throughout these pages. Yet, in some fragile poetic irony, just as this book was headed in one firm direction, my life—and therefore these pages—unexpectedly went another.

If you read my book *Known*, you might recognize the name of my best friend of twenty-five years, Jenn Ohlinger. Jenn was my ride-or-die, my go-to person in crisis, my first call when anything good or hard happened, and the emergency contact on my kids' school forms, their guardian in my will. For a quarter of a century, Jenn and I stewarded ministries, marriages, miscarriages, and the raising of families. We shared inside jokes and side-eyed glances that would cause the other to immediately burst into uproarious laughter. We spoke or texted nearly every single day for over two decades. For all those years, we tended to all the momentous minutiae that add up to a deep soul friendship.

And then, at the end of 2022, we were forced to steward something new—a sudden goodbye. Jenn died on the winter solstice, the longest night of the year, after just a week on hospice, following her arduous two-year battle with breast cancer.

Just as suddenly, this book could no longer be a *what-happens-when-your-dreams-die* book. These pages, instead, became a journey of loss and fresh grief, a slog through the dark, an attempt to stay awake, a way to put one unsteady foot in front of the other. While writing these words, I have fought to be brave for myself and for my people. I have fought to remain present when I felt like I was evaporating.

And I have fought to stay connected to you.

It's easy to underestimate what loss does to the body and soul, the heaviness of grief, until you're in it. It's easy to feel utterly alone, like no one else in the world can understand the void, the wild exhaustion, the onslaught of complicated emotions and physiological reactions. Grief is harder than anyone will tell you, acute and shocking and messy. You carry grief in your lungs, your limbs, your adrenal system. It makes you vomit and lose sleep.

Grief is also very difficult to find language for, to explain, because it can feel like so many jumbled, opposed, and poignant metaphors or events all at once. Grief is like jumping on a cheerless trampoline, a constant disorientation between adrenaline and gravity. Grief is an empty, dilapidating playground—a sad, stoic icon of lost memories and *what could have been*s. Grief is a firestorm, full of uncontrollable destruction and rage, and simultaneously a mudslide, sloppy, shocking, and unstoppable. Grief is a planet—vast, cold, and mysterious. And grief is somehow also a roly-poly pill bug, often unnoticed by others, armored and earthy.

But you don't know all that until you know it, and once you know it, you wonder if anyone else could possibly understand, since you can barely make sense of it yourself. You can barely identify yourself on the grief map, let alone find language to describe the terrain.

For weeks after Jenn died, I couldn't sleep. A good friend was nursing her newborn twins at the time, so she was often up in the same strange, wee hours. She invited me to text her at 1:00 a.m. or 3:00 a.m. or 5:00 a.m., and she would consistently reply with "Get up and write. You need to be writing."

So that's what I did. I wrote this book in the dark, both figuratively and factually. Through restless, wrestling nights, I tried to find language for the unspeakable, attempted to forge a path through the unknowable. I wrote while waiting for a word from God, who has felt so oddly distant from me this year, even while showing up in wild ways.

Mostly, I wrote for you, so that even as you feel alone, you and I can be alone together.

I wrote these words from my deep abyss of grief because I could not stop thinking about all of us who lose what we love, who are bent over by the heft, the magnitude, of it. I wrote these words as a way to reach through the chasm and confusion so we can find each other, and in the finding, to offer *I know* and *I understand* and *I've got you*. I have felt the solemnity of this sacred task: to become your traveling companion through the dark; to help you encounter, as I have (though not without struggle), God's goodness where it seems like none could or should exist. This has been my undertaking, for me and for you: to find goodness, hope, and God's presence in freshest sorrow and darkest nights.

And as I wrote in the middle of the night, I came to view grief differently: as a paradoxical waking up. In grief, our eyes are blinking, adjusting—not to light but to *night*. In our losses, we are bidden awake to strange darkness and surprising gifts.

So many of us inherited a sort of sunny spirituality, the tendency to avoid darkness, or avoid what the darkness might teach us. But as Barbara Brown Taylor, author and spiritual director, writes,

> The way most people talk about darkness, you would think that it came from a whole different deity, but no. To be human is to live by sunlight and moonlight, with anxiety and delight, admitting limits and transcending them, falling down and rising up. To want a life with only half of these things in it is to want half a life, shutting the other half away where it will not interfere with one's bright fantasies of the way things ought to be.[1]

Did you know that there are at least 153 passages of Scripture about darkness? Yes, in many of them, the darkness is a bad, an evil, or a gloom that God has overcome; Jesus is the Light of the World, after all (John 8:12). Darkness is not dark to him, after all (Psalm 139:12).

But there are others—mysterious passages of Scripture, texts I was not formed in, did not memorize, texts I've never heard preached on—where darkness is a companion (Psalm 88:18), where darkness envelops God's throne (Psalm 97:2), where darkness is good (Genesis 1:18), and where darkness contains treasures (Isaiah 45:3, ESV).

Maybe you find yourself in the dark right now—distressed, disappointed, and deeply confused. You don't see God's light overcoming the darkness, and you certainly aren't finding any treasures in it. You are just trying to survive. You are endeavoring to *not sink* in the dark waters of grief, while overwhelming waves of lost people, pathways, and pipe dreams crash over you. You're fighting fiercely to exist in your skin, to *not* disappear, to screw your faith to the sticking place, while at the same time you feel like you're barely inhabiting your own life, a two-dimensional portrayal of who you used to be.

I know how that feels, friend. You are not alone.

This book is an invitation from one nighttime traveler to another, an opportunity to walk side by side through the darkness, to honor our pain and loss and discover how God shows up in what feels like his absence. By creating space for the worst things we have ever been forced to hold, by forging the darkest paths we have ever tread, I believe we can—we *will*—find glimmers of goodness here.

☽

Grief, and fresh grief in particular, is an uncharitable, unchartable path. It does not follow a pattern, arc, or tidy progression, and I refuse to be reductive or formulaic about pain. Still, I hope you'll allow me to join you as a fellow wanderer through grief's obscurity, one who has walked a piece of the path and discovered some of what is hidden in the landscape. Whether you are grieving the loss of your person, the end of a relationship, the death of a dream, or the vanishing of hope, I hope to offer a rhythm and relationship in our shared experiences of loss. Together we will journey through three occurrences of the dark night: its onset (nightfall), its darkest hour (midnight), and the daring moments of luminosity that emerge *only* as our eyes adjust to deep darkness (night-lights).

I'll do my best to offer us some mile markers along the dim path. If you are feeling a little lost in your dark night or on your grief journey, this book will help you locate yourself and show you an honest way forward through the dark.

We will begin by orienting ourselves to the dark night of the soul. Then we will spend some time in twilight, when we start to realize that we have no power to stop or control the darkness that is coming. Here there is still some light to be found, but we must be sober-minded about the coming night. Then we will move toward dusk, the start of night, when loss and pain become inevitable.

From there, we'll journey cautiously through the darkest part of grief and loss, midnight, where loneliness, heaviness, sleeplessness, and unadulterated sadness live. This is where the path of our journey is not as clear, and we might stumble a bit or lose our way momentarily. My prayer as you travel with me—especially if you find yourself in your own midnight of the soul—is that these chapters will bring you a sense of solidarity and solace, a safe place to bring your raw pain, your grim questions, and your own grappling with God. Nothing you feel or think will surprise me because I have felt it and wrestled it to the ground, too, as you'll find while you read.

This is not a morning book or a sunrise book, so there is not much talk of daybreak in these pages. But even blackest midnight does not last forever. We will make our way, even if a bit wobblingly, to the blue hour—that time just before the gilded light of morning appears. There is hope, however fragile, however weary, in the whispers that dawn is coming.

As we travel through the night together, and as you find your way to the end of this book, it's unlikely that your grief will have gone anywhere. But you will find that you have changed because you have survived something. And nighttime survivors have a way of giving birth to new gifts of creativity, compassion, connection, empathy, meaning, real faith, deep love, healthy boundaries, and a gravitas about what matters in life—what some might call wisdom. You might even discover a miracle along the way: You are healing even as you are hurting.

If you are in the thick of fresh grief, feel free to give yourself permission to simply receive these words, to feel seen and not alone, rather than reflect on them or feel any pressure to manufacture something out of them. If you find yourself with a longing and renewed strength to step forward, either on your own or with a group, you'll find some reflections, considerations, and spiritual practices for the journey in the back of the book. I hope these will add meaning to your spiritual and emotional journey.

So here we go.

I am going to let you in on my process of grief, and fair warning: These pages are filled with a sometimes unrelenting heartache and a painfully honest brawl with God. But they are also filled with my reach for hope and God's presence in absence. In my own darkness, I have found myself surprised by God's love, even when I couldn't feel him, sense him, or hear from him. I believe God longs to meet you in the same way.

In one of C. S. Lewis's earliest works, a fairly unsuccessful mythical poem called *Dymer*, Lewis writes about a man not unlike himself—a brave hero facing a monster. *Dymer*, as Lewis scholar David C. Downing explains, is filled with hints of a classically Lewisian suggestion: "that death may have the power to transform something loathsome into something beautiful."[2]

As we walk together through unspeakable and unknowable things, I can tell you this: If you pay attention, if you wrestle with God, grief can become a garden. There is some goodness to find, though it may be hard to see in the haze of your heartache. Because of Jesus' death and resurrection, the power to transform something loathsome into something beautiful exists. This is who God is. This is what God's Spirit has always done. This is what Jesus will ever do.

•

A friend recently reminded me that light is never really absent. In the arc and turn of Earth, light is simply hidden. The sun is always somewhere, and night always, inextricably, moves toward dawn. Darkness isn't what defines night. The sun's rays are always there, just on the other side of shadow, just on the other side of the moon. As your eyes adjust to the night, as you wade through the dark and wait for daylight to return, may you remember this—where there is a dark night, there are also stars, blinking punctuation marks to light your way.

I want you to know that I do not take your pain lightly. I have poured and prayed over every sentence here, with one goal: that you will encounter God's love in the darkness. I will do my very best to help you find him here.

Aubrey

PART ONE

NIGHTFALL

Earth was a soup of nothingness, a bottomless emptiness, an inky blackness. God's Spirit brooded like a bird above the watery abyss.

GENESIS 1:2, MSG

Are your wonders known in the place of darkness,
or your righteous deeds in the land of oblivion?

PSALM 88:12

A LITURGY FOR WHAT WE LOSE IN THE DARK

We begin with a list of lost things:

dreams
tokens
memories
relationships
hopes
a sure faith

These lost things are more than nouns.
They are verbs and adjectives—telling stories, keeping secrets,
standing as witnesses
to languishing time,
to eras that live and breathe within us.
And of course they do.
We always contain every season.
But some of these seasons, some of these losses,
have left us fragile, fragmented.

And now it is nightfall.
The time of leaning in closely.
The time of closing things down.
The time of whispered goodbyes.
The time of forlorn formlessness.

As we face the coming darkness,
we lift our list of lost things to you, O God.
The God Who Hangs the Moon.
The God Who Flicks On the Stars.
The God Who Sees in the Dark.

Would you, God with Night Vision, scan the universe for our
missing matters?
Please find them, tend to them, and care for them,
as only you can.
We trust that nothing is truly lost with you, in you.

Our hearts are broken from longing for so many precious
lost things.
Once, we were found, but now we are also lost.
So would you, God of Lost Things, come find us
in the descending darkness?

1

ENTER THE DARK

Understanding the Night You Find Yourself In

Someone once said that grief occurs anytime you wish something was more, better, or different. So, in its most basic and ubiquitous form, grief happens when life is not turning out how you expected. Grief isn't limited to loss, or even death. Grief happens anytime you find yourself holding tightly to the precious dust of prayers that never materialized, caring for the cinder of languishing hopes.

We are all tending to ashes of some kind.

My best friend, my ride-or-die of over twenty-five years, is dying of breast cancer. My faith tells me that God could stop it. But God is not stopping it. And since I do not have the power to stop it myself, there is an actual physical ache in my chest. I feel like I'm molting, melting, like my intestines and tendons and soul are spilling out of me. I regularly place my hand on my heart and whisper to myself, "You are safe. You are contained. You are not splattering everywhere."

God also seems distant from me in this season. I don't know what God is doing. Why are God's presence and power sometimes so evident, so palpable that even the most committed doubter couldn't deny his miracle making, yet other times so abstruse, so *not there*? I'll never understand. Theologians say that if I did understand, it wouldn't be God I understood. God, in *being God*, is mysterious, inexplicable, beyond containing with our notions. There's no explaining incomprehensibility, I guess.

So I am meeting with a new spiritual director, Ben, and I'm trying to find my bearings in all this uncertainty, in what is starting to feel like spiritual upheaval, spiritual unravel.

In one of our first sessions together, Ben guides me through an imaginative spiritual practice he calls "Jesus on the Bridge." I feel dubious as I watch him walk across his office to a CD player (of all things), press an open button (of all things), and put in a CD (of all things). I move rapidly from dubious to cynical when *nature sounds* begin to play a bit too enthusiastically over the weary speaker system. I privately ask God to remove my cynicism. I want to enter this experience with an open heart.

I close my eyes, adjust myself on Ben's couch, and place my two feet firmly on the carpet beneath me. I square my shoulders, put my hand over my heart, pull in a deep breath, then exhale my skepticism in order to *be here now*. Gratefully, this time I find the birdsong peaceful. The crunch of gravel relaxing. The sound of a rushing river centering. Soon, I am able to be present in this moment. But then Ben invites me to "sit with Jesus on a bridge over a river" in my imagination, and I startle, almost freezing at the invitation.

I don't know if you've walked through a spiritual exercise like this before, something intended to ignite your spiritual imagination. These practices can be transformational. The Spirit of God tends to show up with so much love in moments like these. But with my anticipatory grief over losing Jenn, and what feels like spiritual darkness crowding around me, this kind of ask is excruciating. Lately, I struggle anytime I am asked to "picture" Jesus. Other spiritual mentors have prompted me to imagine myself sitting on Jesus' lap or leaning against his frame in a field of wildflowers. I have friends who love imagining that they are sitting on a park bench with Jesus. I just can't do it. It's weird. It makes me cringe. There's some block there, some sort of wall that keeps me from whatever spiritual illumination is supposed to happen.

So today, when Ben asks me to picture Jesus on the bridge just sitting with me, having fun with me, and making me feel loved, I get frustrated. *This won't work*, I want to grind out. Instead, I fight back tears. I am bone-weary from asking God to show up, to hear me, to do something.

Have you felt this spiritual ache too? Maybe you didn't know what you were experiencing because it's been so confusing, so incomprehensible, so *different*. This season of darkness might even make it feel like you've been abandoned by God.

Maybe life has turned out differently than you imagined. Maybe someone spoke a prophecy over you that hasn't come true. Maybe you feel too broken to dream. Maybe you prayed and prayed but have found no answer, no solace. Maybe your faith is changing and that is terrifying. Maybe grief has stolen your joy. Maybe your losses are too much to bear. Maybe you are fatigued from asking God your questions.

This searing feeling of loss, this wondering where God is, and this exhaustion from begging him to show up time and time again with what feels like no response have a name—*the dark night of the soul.*

☾

When our spiritual path suddenly darkens and our conflicting emotions battle for supremacy, finding language for the disorientation helps us plot our course. If we can make the tiniest semblance of sense in what feels senseless, then we can stretch our legs out in it, explore a bit. Like knowing your coordinates on a map, if you can locate yourself even when you feel lost, you can get your bearings.

And bearings are the difference between survival and overwhelm.

So what is the dark night of the soul?

I mentioned the phrase to a friend once, and he thought I was talking about Batman. "Not *that* Dark Knight," I said, shaking my head and laughing him off.

Beyond the Caped Crusader, we've largely misunderstood the concept, or at least largely misused it, in our current vernacular. We've bucketed "the dark night" into a general category with sadness, depression, doubt, or spiritual dryness, which isn't entirely inaccurate, but neither is it the whole picture.

The dark night is a season of spiritual *difficult to see*–ness. It's an experience of God removing the "felt sense" of his presence from you—and doing so on purpose. The dark night is not something we choose. Rather, the dark night *descends.* Night *falls.*

The phrase *the dark night of the soul,* or *la noche oscura,* is credited to St. John of the Cross, a Spanish priest who was deeply influenced by his spiritual mother and mentor, St. Teresa of Ávila. Teresa was a Carmelite prioress and reformer who affectionally referred to John as "half a friar" because he was so short—under five feet.[1] I picture him as a tiny Friar Tuck from Disney's animated *Robin Hood.*

John and Teresa were wildly different, near opposites. Teresa was born into wealth in 1515 during the Spanish Inquisition and raised by a single dad after losing her mom at age twelve; John was born into poverty in 1542 and raised by a single mom after losing his dad at a young age. John was rigorous and highly educated, while Teresa, though educated at home, was deeply self-conscious about her lack of formal, theological education. Still, these two Catholic mystics connected through their deep passion about prayer and formed an incredible co-laboring partnership in ministry (much like Paul with Lydia, Priscilla, and Phoebe).

Teresa's own dark-night journey included intense family conflict, acute self-doubt, severe chronic illness, and such a low sense of worth that she stopped praying for years, something she would come to regret for the rest of her life.[2] Yet, in the midst of her physical, emotional, and spiritual darkness, God drew Teresa into deeper intimacy with him and gave her more confidence in her life's calling. As she witnessed corruption in the Catholic Church, she did not shut down or turn away: She chose to stay connected to the church and work for change. She founded several convents as part of the Carmelite order, a return to the older desert way of solitude, simplicity, and prayer—and a rejection of what she was seeing in the church around her. Many monasteries were also founded because of Teresa's decades of reform.

St. John's dark night came when, just a year after joining Teresa's reforming work, he was abducted by an opposing Carmelite faction and kept as their prisoner. He was thrown into solitary confinement, badly abused, never allowed to bathe or clean himself, and taken out only once a day on a lead.[3] I once read that John was rarely fed, maybe being offered one sardine once a day. While imprisoned, John had a powerful encounter with God. This experience led him to write a poem, "The Spiritual Canticle," and eventually another, "The Dark Night of the Soul."

According to both John and Teresa, the dark night is something God does deliberately—and not only deliberately, but *lovingly*. The dark night is intended to bring us freedom from our false attachments and idols and deepen our intimacy with divine Love—to help us know our unshakable identity as the beloved[4] while helping us better love others.

The dark night's goal is all about that: love and loving.

To be honest, I haven't internalized this yet, nor am I sure I believe it.

Why would the God you have communed with your entire life suddenly seem absent or distant in the most fragile of circumstances? What sort of loving God pulls his presence from you right when you need him? And how is that supposed to draw you closer? Isn't that just a childish game of hide-and-seek?

Scripture promises that God neither leaves us nor forsakes us (Deuteronomy 31:6). So in the dark night, that must mean that God never *removes his actual presence*.

"The Dark Night of the Soul," then, is better translated by tracing the etymology of a word in John's Spanish title, "Noche oscura del alma"—"The *Obscure* Night of the Soul." *Obscure* because during the dark night, the receiver can rarely decipher what God is doing; God's plan and presence are hidden and out of view. (For a primer on the dark night, see appendix A, "What Is the Dark Night of the Soul?")

If there is anything typical in a dark night of the soul, it is just that—the sense of nonsense, the *what-in-the-world-is-God-doing?* of it all. It is nearly impossible to ascertain what God is up to or determine where he is leading.

And since I cannot currently make sense of this season I am walking through, and because I have no idea how dark my night will grow, I am meeting with my spiritual director to find some modicum of understanding, to provide at least a glimpse of a path forward through the waning light.

☽

Back in Ben's office, I am still upset, worn out from willing myself to "be with Jesus on the bridge." I don't know if Ben notices my anxiety or if this is part of the spiritual exercise's purpose. But he asks me, as I sit on this imaginary bridge, to "stand up and walk to a beach" in my imagination.

"Ask God to meet you there," he adds.

The music soundtrack shifts now. I stretch my legs and shift my body, trying to be present again. Soon I'm in an ocean scene by night. I hear the tide's inhale and exhale, a crackling bonfire. I am suddenly there, walking along the sandy shore.

And that is when a lion appears at my side.

This lion is alert, a protector. But also somehow warm and inviting, with big, golden paws: a wild, tangled mane; and a coat so warm and smooth I can almost feel it.

The lion's pace is slow, and I sense it telling me to go as slow as I need to. *I will keep pace with you.* This beast is not scary; it's just sort of *around. There. Here. Now.* Weaving in and out of my path on the sand as the stars shimmer above us—always keeping watch, keeping time, keeping steady with me on the beach. Sometimes its large paws playfully pat at the ocean tide. Sometimes the lion plods deliberately behind me. All the while, I sense that patient, unbothered steadiness: *I can go as slow as you need me to.*

I understand that this is counterintuitive even as I experience it—after all, we should move at God's pace, not the other way around, right? Isn't that what faithful Christians do? And yet, somehow, I know this is simultaneously true: If God is willing to go as slow as we need to through the thick fog of night, that means we do not have to rush to solve it or emerge from it or even "win" it.

God is never in a hurry as we are hurried, because hurry is the opposite of love. Though I am in a rush to decipher the dark night's mysteries, though I am desperate to time jump to ten years from now when this year is a distant memory and I've made sense of it and learned the lessons from it—

God is neither rushed nor delayed.

The dark night is slow work.

Ben interrupts my meandering thoughts. "Aubrey, if there is anything you want to say to God while you are on the beach, feel free to voice that aloud or say it silently in your mind."

I choose the silent route. *Okay, Lion,* I think to myself, or maybe I think these things toward God, hurl them near God, bleed them out in the direction of God. *If you are keeping pace with me, I have some . . . thoughts.*

If you are keeping pace with me, if you are truly here, then why does it feel like you're abandoning me in my darkest hour—right when I have needed your comfort and your peace the most? I am so angry at you. Am I repellent? Have I disappointed you? Have I done something wrong? Are you punishing me for something? Or am I delusional, and this is simply how it feels when life gets hard? And how long will this distance, this silence, last? Are you even listening to me? This is too much, God. I am exhausted.

I pause my diatribe briefly to gather my thoughts and then press on. *My faith feels so frail, so small. Can this minuscule belief be enough for you? Because it doesn't feel enough for me.*

This spiritual practice may be inviting me to use my holy imagination, but we are never asked to playact with God. Faith never requires pretending. So I roll my ankles, stretch my neck, and pause before naming, before *admitting*, the last of my questions.

Is your arm so short that you cannot stop cancer?
Are you weak?
Are you even able?
Are my prayers just an afterthought to you? A joke?
Because I have been asking you to heal Jenn, and I have been asking you to show up with me, and your silence is callous.

I feel electric as I finally let my raw, red, inflamed laments unfurl. These are the real ones, the questions I am afraid of, the ones that have been thrumming within me for some time now, beating against the edges of my bones, hammering under the pores of my skin. Today, they have become a lit fuse racing toward me, ready to explode. My lament is a bid, a fight for my relationship with God. And I need him to answer, or I might not survive the dark night.

Still, with what little mustard seed I can muster, wrung out after this audacious questioning, I risk one more plea:

God, please. Please. Please. Please come be with me again. Please be who you say you are. Please keep loving me. Please don't leave me alone in this.

In your own dark night, you probably have some unspoken questions, the subterranean ones. You are not alone in that. It's not faithless to ask your cavernous questions. It's a bold act of worship because lament requires intimacy. There are exceptions, of course, but we don't often get meaningfully angry at or profoundly frustrated with people we care little to nothing about, right? Absent relationship, we are indifferent, or the anger is passing. If you've got some spitfire for Jesus, I say, set the night ablaze.

•

I am exhausted emotionally, ready to be done, just as Ben begins to wind down the exercise. The music from the CD shifts again, this time to the rushing sound of wind blowing. Ben asks me, "Is there anyplace else you'd like to go before we end this exercise?"

I inhale deeply, unclenching and stretching out my fingers. I've been holding them in fists and didn't even realize it. I allow myself this final moment and end atop a cliff, like a Jane Austenian heroine. The wind is blowing my long skirts and tangling my hair. It is drizzling, and I am looking out over the gray ocean. That ocean is a world, a realm, a veil, a cosmos. That ocean is the cloud of unknowing, where I currently exist. Jenn will soon be on the other side of that ocean. The lion is at the bottom of my cliff, and somehow the lion is also the ocean.

Ben finally turns off the CD, and my eyes are puffy from tears. He looks at me with concern, so I try to explain. I tell him about the lion, about our conversation, or rather, my word vomit *at* the lion. "I worry," I try to explain, "about how God will or won't respond to my questions. But I also worry that I can't envision Jesus with me. And even when I do, God appears in my imagination as nothing more than a lion. Like I can't get beyond some childish, C. S. Lewisian version of God."

Ben, like the lion, is unrushed, and his pause is taxing to my impatient heart. He eventually replies softly, "Maybe. But what if this is how God is inviting you to see him? There's no shame in that, Aubrey. What is it about the lion that God wants you to notice?"

When I reflect on that question a few days later, I jot down some bullet notes in my journal to describe the lion in my vision:

- big paws—protection
- warm coat—safety and comfort
- wild mane—uncontrollable, undomesticated, untamed
- beating heart—alive and real
- king—predator and protector
- pacer—friend in the dark night

Later, much later, in a future spiritual-direction session, God will invite me to see Jesus as my older brother and my best friend. But for now, I am coming to terms with something: This lion is my dark-night companion. I have been looking for God, and I suppose God has revealed himself. Just not as I expected.

I don't know how dark your night will become, how loud the din of darkness will grow. But I know that God is not yanking you up some mechanical ladder of spiritual growth or rushing you past a finish line of pain. And I know you are not going backward. You are not moving too slow.

God is protective of and patient with you as you stop along the shore of confusing loss, kneel in the sand, and let your tears and groans keep stride with the broiling, roaring, dark ocean.

2

TWILIGHT ON THE HORIZON

As Loss Comes Close

"I thought I'd be there by now."

My friend mutters that statement, that *announcement*, as a nonchalant afterthought over lunch. As if it were so normal, in between bites of Caesar salad, to admit that one's path has become unexpected, painful, thwarted, disrupted.

But the thing is, it *is* normal. I have had this identical conversation multiple times lately—in coffee shops and at restaurants, across various tables from various acquaintances, friends, and family members. Somewhere along the journey, they took a wrong turn; the terrain became rocky; they looked around and realized they didn't know where they were or maybe even who they were.

Many of us have dreams that have slowly melted over the years, candle wax against the flame of life. Many of us are standing over coffins of hopes deferred, clutching tender lists of disappointments close to our chests. Somewhere along the way, a vague darkness, an imprecise disenchantment with life, began descending. But it wasn't dramatic or shocking. It was slow, commonplace, quotidian, nearly unnoticed. Nothing is *wrong*, exactly. We think we *should* be fine. Yet something deep and true in us knows we aren't.

We thought we'd be there by now. But we aren't.

In this twilight before the dark, when light still filters through, we experience an early, prescient grief, almost formless. Though we may not feel like we're completely surrounded by darkness, we certainly sense it creeping over the horizon of our souls. It's not necessarily a sharp or deep pain, more like a nebulous disruption. Our stomachs flip; our anxiety spikes. Something is off, and yet everything still looks okay. Everything's holding together, even if by taut strings that feel close to snapping.

After lunch with my friend, I'm driving to a doctor's appointment for this very reason—this *something-is-wrong-but-nothing-is-wrong* twilight mood. When I made the appointment online, the intake form asked some version of "What do you most want to focus on during today's appointment?" I sighed aloud, shrugged my shoulders, and started typing, "I don't know. A potential midlife crisis? I can't seem to handle my best friend's prognosis?"

I wanted to add, "Basically, it's rough out here in these streets."

Instead, I hit the delete button. Delete. Delete. Deleeeeeeete. I sat there in front of my computer screen for a breath or two, thinking. Then finally placed my fingers back on the keyboard, typing each next letter deliberately: "Mostly, I don't feel like myself."

Which is maybe just another way of saying, *I thought I'd be there by now.*

As I write this, I am almost forty-five years old. Some of this spiritual twilight can probably be chalked up to midlife, but it's honestly not the *math* of my age. I enjoy the gift of maturity and the delicious anticipation of new seasons. I've just had this vague sense of discontent, disruption, an *ache* for the past several years—*I am not where I thought I'd be by now.* I am not settled in my career. I have not saved enough money. I have not given my children the life lessons I planned to. I am not as healthy as I would like. I don't have enough time, or at least I haven't scheduled my time in the right ways. I haven't accomplished all I thought I would.

So I am visiting my doctor because I am experiencing a hazy sunset of the soul, a dimming daylight of the spirit, an obscure disquieting of the heart. And I need as much help as I can get.

The other reason for this appointment is of course Jenn. Jenn, with little time left. Cancer, taking too much of it. Jenn is almost forty-three. Her life, her husband's life, their three sons' lives are not where they thought they'd be right now.

I likely won't talk to my doctor about what God will or won't do for Jenn, how God seems to be ignoring my prayers for her healing. But I do plan to at least mention the emotional overwhelm of midlife and the pain of watching my best friend fade away.

All this brings me to you. Where are you right now?

Maybe you sense the darkness descending. Maybe your path isn't going the way you planned. Maybe you are tending to some unexpected ashes. On a scale of *I-am-not-where-I-thought-I'd-be-by-now* to *I-am-so-lost-I-can-barely-breathe*, where do you find yourself? What have you lost? What disruption are you facing? However you answer, wherever you are, you are not alone.

When I think about my own answers to those questions, there is so much I don't know yet. All I know is that the light may not have fully disappeared from the horizon, but I'm moving inextricably toward some kind of spiritual blackout.

I leave my doctor's office without mentioning any of this. As planned, I talk with her mostly about my midlife malaise and how difficult this season has been and is rapidly becoming. She recommends vitamin D and some follow-up lab work and suggests I talk to a therapist. The appointment is helpful in its simplicity. Much feels complicated these days; it's nice to leave with straightforward instructions.

☾

As a distraction from life's confusion, I have recently picked up painting as a hobby. I am a terrible painter, and I don't say that from any internalized imposter syndrome; this is a sober-minded assessment. But I paint, partly, for that very reason, *because* I am so unskilled. It's a place in life where I don't have to perform, overthink, or be "on." I can enjoy the creative process, the playfulness, without any pressure to succeed, manage, or do it "right." These days, I am finding that my soul needs more and more set-aside spaces like this.

One evening, I attend a paint-in-the-dark class at one of those paint-and-sip places. All of us in attendance gather around long tables in a sort of communal dining experience, but with canvases and paint palettes prefilled with bright colors. Our instructor turns down the studio lights, leaving on only a few dim lamps. She gives us an example to follow—a mountain range at sunset—but adds, "Trust your instincts. Paint whatever and however you feel led. Let go. Whatever you do, don't try to force an outcome."

We spend the next two hours creating in twilight. I giggle my way through, making awkward, uneven brushstrokes, splattering paint on myself. At the end of class, our instructor goes for A Big Reveal—with a dramatic flourish, she switches on a black light, and our canvases are like northern lights—incandescent blues, greens, pinks, and ultraviolets—in the dark studio. When my eyes adjust to my own canvas in front of me, I find myself grinning at a sad trio of trippy and tragic triangles. My glow-in-the-dark painting is so pitiable, I can't help but adore it.

Maybe this is the way night falls. You can't guess how dark the night will become, can't know how opaque things will grow or what you will discover as the light fades. What seems to be asked of us here, in this early darkness, is to release the outcome. Concede.

My best friend is dying, and life is listless and disappointing, and humans are just so, so fragile. We all thought we'd arrive at that elusive *there*, but we haven't. We are all just realizing the arrival itself is a fallacy.

Whatever darkness looms for you, whatever disruption is leaving you sleepless, whatever loss is taking shape, I want to tell you that it will be okay, that you'll make meaningful breakthroughs here. But I also think it might be a very long time before it is okay. It might be hazy for a while before the path becomes clear. The darkness that will descend is not a joke. You will have to struggle and fight and rally whatever spiritual and emotional muscles you've ever worked, and even the ones you haven't trained yet. But perhaps the hardest exertion will come from learning to let go—from unclenching your fists in order to surrender to whatever God is doing in the dark.

As twilight signals the impending night, we can clutch frantically to the remains of what is slipping through our fingers anyway, or we can open our hands—releasing our fears, our unknown paths, and our misplaced ideas *about* God to God.

Life's disappointments are gravitational, often pulling you into the dark night with no way to stop what's coming. You might be tempted to control the night, rush past it, or pretend it isn't happening. Don't. Though it may seem counterintuitive, don't ignore the twilight. Face it. Explore it. With as much curiosity and openness as you can muster, paint in the coming dark.

New Testament writer James says something similar: "Consider it a sheer gift, friends, when tests and challenges come at you from all sides. You know that under pressure, your faith-life is forced into the open and shows its true colors. So don't try to get out of anything prematurely. Let it do its work so you become mature and well-developed, not deficient in any way" (James 1:2-4, MSG).

Keep yourself open to what this evening season may reveal, what it has to teach you, what God wants to unveil in it. Let it do its work, though the work may be awfully painful.

You may just discover some kind of afterglow for the night ahead.

3

THE OBSCURITY OF DUSK

When God Seems Hidden

It's a crisp fall morning, and I've woken up before the boys. As I gingerly tiptoe downstairs, I note every footfall, register every squeak of the floorboards, and pray a soundless plea. *Please don't let anyone wake up yet. I need this time. I need this time so desperately.*

It has become my ritual, my mode of survival—to light a candle, do some reading and journaling, and drink a large cup of coffee (make that *several* large cups of coffee) before my house awakens.

I slip into a worn-out mustard-yellow leather armchair in my reading room, open to a blank page in my journal, and scrawl my usual question.

God, where are you?

I have not been able to sense God's presence with me for so long now. I have been asking this question repeatedly for months and months and months, and I am bone-weary from not hearing an answer.

Spiritual dusk, the time of night after twilight, is when we first start to feel like the presence of God is hidden, veiled, pulled back for some unknown, frustrating reason. It's not yet completely dark. There is still some light, though fading. But these are the moments on your darkening path when you must squint to see the way forward.

In this season of disorientation, I don't know what God is doing exactly, but I have a sense of God's intentional hiddenness, God's purposeful obscurity. God is hiding his face from me. Why? My theological fill-in-the-blank answer is that God wants to transform me somehow. But mostly, I have questions. No answers seem to be enough.

Yet Scripture does give us examples of God's obscurity . . . God concealing his glory or appearing in a dark cloud or in murky darkness (emphases added):

> The people stood far off, while Moses drew near to the *thick darkness* where God was.
>
> EXODUS 20:21, ESV

> "You came near and stood at the foot of the mountain, while the mountain burned with fire to the heart of heaven, *wrapped in darkness, cloud, and gloom.*"
>
> DEUTERONOMY 4:11, ESV

"The *secret things* belong to the LORD our God, but the things that are revealed belong to us and to our children forever, that we may do all the words of this law."

DEUTERONOMY 29:29, ESV

How long, O LORD? Will you forget me forever?
How long will you *hide* your face from me?

PSALM 13:1, ESV

It is the glory of God to *conceal* a matter;
to search out a matter is the glory of kings.

PROVERBS 25:2

Truly, you are a God who *hides himself*,
O God of Israel, the Savior.

ISAIAH 45:15, ESV

"He reveals deep and *hidden things*;
he knows what is in the darkness,
and the light dwells with him."

DANIEL 2:22, ESV

I'll be the first to tell you that best-practice biblical exegesis requires more than a simple word study or a few verses as proof of concept, but a sense of God's hiddenness can be found throughout the Scriptures, throughout history, throughout our spiritual formation. I suppose I'm reminding us both of that, me and you, so that we don't feel so alone or confused when God's presence seems more like absence. There is some sort of divine precedence here. But the *why* and the *where is God* of it all? That I still can't answer.

I've been in spiritual seasons adjacent to this one before, seasons of lament brought on by illness and grief. Yet even in those seasons, I knew God's *withness* with me. I knew Immanuel's presence. I felt God's comfort.

This is different.

Something has shifted.

My relationship with God used to be different. Easier, perhaps. More *naïve* in the best sense—trusting, guileless, childlike. I had a clear vision of what God was doing in my life, where God was leading. I had certainty, clarity. But this year, God seems to be obscuring my lucidity, and doing so *intentionally*.

I've found myself calling this *a breadcrumb year*. Like Hansel and Gretel, I am following a trail of crumbs, uncertain if it will lead to more loss or more hope. And God is being enigmatic, giving me appetizers, not the meal—crumbs, but not the whole loaf. God is giving me pieces, not the puzzle. God is giving me glimpses, not the view. In this breadcrumb year, hope comes in fragments.

This mystery of what God is up to while God seems to have withdrawn from me—while also somehow beckoning me to follow him on some pathless path—doesn't *feel* particularly enjoyable. My faith feels like a pile of breadcrumbs, and I don't have much wherewithal to think rightly about what God is doing or not doing as I prepare to say goodbye to my best friend of a quarter of a century. As I find myself in the confusion of dusk.

And look, I'm a pastor. I know that spiritual transformation doesn't happen in comfort. But knowing something, even believing something, doesn't make it easy to internalize. When something doesn't *feel* true, sometimes the only thing we can do is look at what has been true before. We must remember in the dark what we knew in the light. Remember under the moon what we knew in sunnier seasons. We even remember nights we've been in before—maybe not as dark, maybe not as long—and how we stepped out into daylight again to discover that God was with us the whole time. Relying on what we know about God's character, goodness, and revelation gives us sustenance for the journey ahead. Intentionally recalling how God has worked in the past helps us make out his presence in our hazy now. Looking at the lives of other followers of God throughout history gives us hope as we see how God has used the obscure evening before.

I suppose that's why I keep showing up each morning to this armchair, tracing the same well-worn path in my journal that I have all year. It's all I know to do. My mornings with God in this silent season aren't awe-inspiring or productive. Mostly, my time with God is simple repetition, but the repetition has become a practice in spiritual survival. St. John of the Cross says faith is a "habit of the soul."[1] So this is my habit of faith each morning: I read a psalm, a liturgy, a book on darkness, the poetry of Rosemerry Wahtola Trommer, or a lament from Natasha Sistrunk Robinson's *Voices of Lament*. And I wait for God to show up.

God, for some reason, just keeps *not* showing up. But I am here, asking, *God, where are you?* and choosing to seek him even if I'm not sure I'll find him.

This is the strange thing about the dark night: It somehow obscures us from connecting with God while drawing us deeper into desire for that connection. The Absence, the Unknowing, the Pulling Away, it all serves as a kind of magnet pulling us toward divine Love.

At least that's what I am telling myself.

I suppose in my daily armchair habit each morning, I'm desperately reaching out for Jesus' robe in the darkness. Mostly, I am crying out, *God, I don't know where you are in this obscurity, but please do not let me go.* Mostly, I'm reminding my soul that he won't. God has found me before. We have found each other.

Remember this, O my soul—
even in the evening when finding is so elusive.

☽

There's an account in Scripture, in the book of Acts, about the apostle Paul's own dark night. Luke's second scroll tells it like this:

> Paul and his companions traveled throughout the region of Phrygia and Galatia, having been kept by the Holy Spirit from preaching the word in the province of Asia. When they came to the border of Mysia, they tried to enter Bithynia, but the Spirit of Jesus would not allow them to. So they passed by Mysia and went down to Troas. During the night Paul had a vision of a man of Macedonia standing and begging him, "Come over to Macedonia and help us." After Paul had seen the vision, we got ready at once to leave for Macedonia, concluding that God had called us to preach the gospel to them.
>
> ACTS 16:6-10

Maybe you notice a repeated refrain:

"*Having been kept* by the Holy Spirit from preaching the word [there] . . ."

"The Spirit of Jesus *would not allow them* to . . ."

Paul and his crew were trying to follow their calling, their mission, yet God thwarted their efforts. God changed their direction. God stopped them in their tracks. God blocked their goal. They thought their feet would take them one way, but the Spirit of Jesus had other plans.

This passage of Scripture almost reads like a cosmic joke, a deistic pinball machine. God was obscuring Paul's path, even as he was inviting the apostle to follow sightlessly. Paul was given a dream, *a vision*, but he did not have a map. Still, Paul took one step of faith at a time while God moved him in unexpected, tedious, and seemingly ridiculous directions.

And yet.

What we see in Paul's story is often what we cannot see in our own, especially when we find ourselves in the middle of an obscure evening. God is at work, even when the path is dim. God is doing something, *something good*, even when we can't see clearly. God's past faithfulness—in Scripture, in our own stories, in the stories of other fellow travelers—can give us something to hold on to when our own belief feels hard.

All along, God was awakening Paul from his former naïveté, exploding out of the boxes Paul had placed him in. God used this journey, in all its disorientation, to reveal that he works in ways bigger than the apostle might have imagined, in and through people he might not have imagined: in Gentiles and in women, outside the institution, outside the religious elite. Paul dreamt of a Macedonian man but was eventually led to Lydia, who became one of the first female leaders of the early church. In this way, God's obscurity served as Paul's invitation into an entirely new trajectory, one where he would co-labor with women for the gospel as he continued to preach that gospel to Gentiles.

Perhaps for us, like for Paul and his companions, every *God, where are you?* is a step toward greater goodness, meaning, depth.

I cling to my tentative hypothesis that in the night we are being invited into transformation. But I can't quite land on my thesis because the darkness doesn't feel particularly helpful or transformative. Mostly, the dusk is presenting a harrowing question: *Can I fumble forward in faith, even if I cannot find the place where God is hiding?*

God is up to something, even as we search for him in the obscurity of dusk. But it's something many of us weren't prepared for in our spiritual formation or church upbringing. In his hiddenness, God is inviting us to release certainty, which is scary.

We are asked, instead, to embrace faith, which is scarier.

•

My boys wake up for school and bound loudly down the stairs. Over the years, their little baby steps have become stomping giant footfalls, difficult to ignore or pray through. So I close my journal. Get up from my chair. Go back to life. Make breakfast. Get dressed. Put on makeup. The clock demands we move forward. Daily routines wait for no one. We can't stay stuck forever. We have facts to attend to—bills to pay, meals to eat, library books to return, kids to take to school, jobs to focus on.

Later that day, at one of my jobs, I spend some time interviewing author and Bible teacher Beth Moore. As we chat, she speaks of her own darkness, of great losses and unconscionable tragedies. "The loss is never, never, never worth it," she pronounces sagely. "But it will matter. God will make it matter." She speaks, too, of a habit of the soul that she turns to in the obscurity, much like my armchair *God, where are you?*s: If she goes even two or three days without sensing God's presence, she is immediately on her face, begging God to return.[2]

After the interview, as the crisp fall afternoon descends into an even cooler fall evening, my husband (Kevin) and I meet up with some dear friends for dinner. I've heard it said that if we are to understand shalom, we will understand it at a table.[3] And I get a glimpse of biblical shalom—wholeness, flourishing, delight, peace, wellness—whenever we break bread with Linda and Daniel.

Tonight we have chosen Korean barbecue at Mr. Kimchi, one of our favorite dining establishments in Chicagoland. We eat bulgogi and galbi with banchan like white rice, kimchi, and fish cakes. We slurp spicy tofu soup and sample tiny sips of sweet, syrupy soju. We eat until we are overstuffed and a little bit giggly. We laugh and we cry.

Linda and Daniel tell us their Hmong family-origin stories, mostly lost or intentionally hidden and still being found. Stories of immigrating, of war, of soldiering, of losing loved ones to IED explosions, of gathering with other Hmong people to try to make sense of their shared tragedy and lost narratives.

We listen, Kevin and I, because we have much to learn and lament. Then, after some time, we begin to trade stories about the hardships of leading postpandemic churches. We lament other losses too. We toast to family members who have died, friendships that have ended, midlife crises that seem to never end.

Our waiter sits down to join the conversation for a bit. We ask where he is from. Seoul. I notice his shirt has a moon and bunny on it and ask him about something I read recently from Eastern folklore: the moon rabbit, akin to the West's man in the moon. He tells me that in some versions of the tale, the moon rabbit holds a mortar and pestle, pounding moon cakes. In others, the moon rabbit holds the elixir of life or a pot of honey, representing rebirth.

Later, as Kevin and I drive home, I think that if there can be honey on the moon, new life birthed at night, then perhaps this can be true as well: Though darkness is certainly gloom, it is also a womb. And as with most birth pangs, bearing down deep and gripping desperately to hope, even as it evades your grip, are the requirements. The delicate bones in my fingers might break from the grasping, my knuckles pale from the exertion, but in my fraught search for hope in the dark, if I squeeze my eyes just so, I realize today has been filled with breadcrumbs:

- a quiet morning,
- hot coffee,
- space for journaling,
- clocks ticking,
- boys buoying,
- prophetic Bible teachers speaking truth,
- spicy tofu,
- sweet soju,
- stories exchanged and held,
- shared suffering, and
- life-giving friendships.

At least for today, I have part of the answer to my question—*God, where are you?*

God is in the obscurity of dusk, dropping crumbs of hope from his fingertips. God is on the moon, holding a jar of honey.

☾

The nightfall is luminous with offerings, but the diminishing light may become so dismal, so opaque, that it will feel excruciatingly tedious to find any hints of goodness here in the obscurity. (See appendix B for a breadcrumb-of-hope exercise that can help you see through the dark.) The unbearable nature of God's silence, the agonizing frustration of God's hiddenness, is enough to cloud your confidence.

Why does God use the dark night to transform us when it seems like he could use something less painful, less confusing? I don't know. I'm just trying to stay put. Show up. And keep looking for God, though I cannot see.

4

THE DIMLY LIT PATH

Persisting When You Can't See the Way Forward

It's nearing Thanksgiving, and a dear friend has sent me a decorative wooden gnome for the holidays. You know the type: all beard, no eyes, and tall, pointy hat. Basically just one tchotchke-triangle made of wood or plush.

Something in me despises this gnome. I feel deep outrage *at the gnome*. I love the friend who sent it to me, so I am committed to finding a place for the little wooden figurine, but its presence is a land mine.

I place it on my fireplace mantel but don't like it there. I move it to a windowsill but hate it there. I try a ledge, a countertop, a shelf. I keep moving it around the house, trying to find a place where I will feel settled about it. And just when I think I've gotten over my strange revulsion, I'll turn a corner, spy the little gnome again, and internally explode with irrational fury.

But I don't want to throw the gnome away. Something in me is super curious about what's behind my reaction. *Why am I so annoyed?*

At first, I assume my resentment is due to the ubiquitous nature of gnomes—they are in every store and available for every holiday. So, sort of like a delicious meal you've eaten too many times, they are bland, tedious, a bit repulsive to me. But I don't think that's it.

I consider whether my problem with the gnome is the actual design itself—its lack of beauty, originality, and decorum. *Maybe this gnome offends my artistic sensibilities.* But I am the kind of person who decorates my house with a Mickey Mouse Christmas Village for the holidays, so that cannot be the issue.

I finally discover the source of my irrational gnome rage when my young nephews come to visit us for their fall break.

The boys love being outside in the Chicago cold and spend their entire time here in motion: raking leaves, running through our neighborhood, using our leaf blower. One morning they are outside hunting for lost treasures in the leaf piles in our backyard while I stay in the kitchen sipping coffee and making them breakfast. After a few minutes, they come barging through the back door, voices filled with urgency and excitement as they shout, "Look, Auntie Aubrey! Look!"

I walk over to them to get a better view of their discovery. To my horror, my youngest nephew is holding the severed head of a small bird. The little bird head is just resting there in his cupped hands, staring up at me, though not actually staring because it is dead, obviously. Also, it doesn't have eyeballs. The thing is perfectly intact, as if it never had a body to begin with.

My nephew stands there holding this little bird head while both boys beam up at me. It's not the reaction they want, but I scream and make them drop it outside immediately, then rush them inside to scour their hands with soap and detergent and any other cleaning agent I can find. At which point they both start crying. So the day isn't off to a great start.

I should probably bury the head in the backyard, let nature do its thing. But I put on disposable kitchen gloves and place the tiny bird's head into a Ziploc bag, then into a grocery bag, then into a garbage bag, and then into the garbage bin outside, where I also throw the gloves away. Then I head back into the house to wash my own hands and comfort the boys.

Oddly, it is right here in my garage, as I walk away from the garbage bins, a bit shaky from revulsion, where I realize the source of my anger about the gnome.

It's grief.

Jenn is rapidly decreasing. God is not answering our prayers for healing. I'm not angry about some dumb decorative wooden gnome. I am angry that dreams die, that our hearts get crushed, and that plans we make seem foolish in light of how life unfolds. I am angry that some prayers seem to hit some invisible ceiling when other prayers are answered miraculously. I am mostly angry that my best friend in the entire world is dying, that God is nowhere to be found in it. I am afraid and alone. And I am angry that the calendar keeps moving forward and I can't stop forward motion, just as I cannot stop cancer from spreading or precious birds from dying.

The gnome, not unlike this weird bird head, in all its *not right*–ness and *out of place*–ness, just happens to be an outlet for my anger and sorrow.

As the familiar proverb says, "Hope deferred makes the heart sick" (Proverbs 13:12). This is true in any kind of loss—the loss of dreams, of justice, of a job, of health, of a relationship, of freedom, of your person. Loss is an intruder, offending and disrupting our ideas about how life should go. We might act like we're okay, but instead we're just heartsick and angry at how weird and sad and strangely out of place the whole thing makes us feel.

No one wants to stay angry at a silly gnome forever. We need to throw away the dead bird's head, because it certainly doesn't belong in a child's hand. But where do we take other intruders? Loss isn't going away. Disappointments won't end. What do we do with them? And what about our unwelcome anger, sadness, and grief? Where do we take those when God feels elusive? When our hearts are sick and hope feels gone and God seems far, how do we not just give up searching for him? Why should we even bother?

☽

In Luke 11, Jesus tells a story about someone banging on his friend's door at midnight, asking for some loaves of bread. Until this year, I don't think I would have noticed the midnight setting of Jesus' teaching.

Jesus starts this story by saying, essentially, "Look, your friend is obviously going to get annoyed because it's midnight and his kids are already asleep. He's in his pajamas and robe, streaming his favorite show, just trying to relax with the little bit of alone time he finally has. He doesn't want to have to get up off the couch and go unlock the door. He'd also have to search the pantry to even find the bread." It seems like Jesus is about to share the man's response as "Sorry, not sorry . . . no bread for you."

But then Jesus surprises his audience with a twist ending: "Even though he will not get up and give you the bread because of friendship, yet because of your *shameless audacity* he will surely get up and give you as much as you need" (Luke 11:8, emphasis added).

Because of your annoying persistence, your friend will get out of bed or shove off the couch and shuffle over to the bread cupboard. He'll get you all the loaves you're asking for.

Jesus tells us to pray with tireless tenacity. He tells us to seek so that we will know his abundant provision rather than fall prey to believing our unmet longings and unanswered prayers are a sign of him not meeting our needs. It can be so easy in the dark night to look at the way life *isn't going* and assume that that means God isn't working, providing, or answering prayers. A counterliturgy to that? Keep asking anyway. Ask expectantly.

Jesus also positions this parable on persistent prayer within something profound: relationship. You can ask of God audaciously because you possess a truly audacious thing—friendship with God. But the bewildering thing is what Jesus says *about* that relationship: *It's not the friendship. That's not why he will give you what you're asking for; it's your impudence.*

When the night is dark, Jesus seems to be saying:

Keep knocking.

Make your faith a verb.

Don't give up.

Don't lose your mettle.

Continue asking for what you need.

There is a line to toe here, of course, lest we begin to think it's on us to say special magic words or perform the perfect dog and pony show to convince God to release some proverbial dangling carrot. Having shameless audacity is not the same thing as striving, earning, or laboring for God's grace. It's a posture of the heart, not a proving of oneself. This story of prayer falls just after Jesus teaches us to pray for daily bread, God's will to be done, and God's Kingdom to come. And though Jesus is certainly encouraging our fearlessness, teaching us to ask God for these things with boldness and bravado, it's ultimately God's grace, God's provision, and God's Kingdom at work.

When the night is so gloomy you can't see the way forward, *even then*, dare to have the nerve to walk over to God's house and make some demands. When your eyes are red and bleary and your knuckles are bloody from the tireless knocking and you're convinced God's either not home or possibly ignoring you, *even then*, keep pounding on God's door.

•

In less than a month from now, Jenn will go on hospice. My secret stasher, my daily-detail confidante who knows all about the dead bird head and my internal gnome conflict, is dying.

On her hospice bed, while breathing from an oxygen tank and comforted by morphine, Jenn giggles and tells me she plans to buy me a monthly gnome subscription before she dies. "Every time a gnome arrives at your doorstep, think of me," she says wryly. Months later, Jenn's husband, Justin, lets me go through her things, and I find a collection of small gnomes in a box marked for me.

I love these gnomes deeply and tenderly.

When dreams die, when our loved ones say goodbye, the dark night gets darker and longer than we are prepared for. There will be so many times we want to give up, to armor ourselves with the belief that if we don't ask, we won't be let down again.

No matter how long your night lasts, or how dim it becomes, Jesus invites you to contend for your faith, to fight courageously when you'd rather fade away.

And somehow, eventually, along the way, loss starts to feel less like an intruder. I won't go so far as to call loss a friend. But you find a place for the gnomes. You wash your hands and are able to find comfort and comfort someone else. And if you don't give up in your darkest hours, if you persist in knocking, in seeking, in asking, in showing up, you find that God eventually puts on his slippers, shuffles to the door, and greets you with warm bread and a side of honey to sustain you until morning.

5

NIGHTTIME LOSSES

Surrendering to the God Who Holds Everything

The first time I learn that God is the Finder of Lost Things, I am in high school and have lost my car keys.

The keys are on a vintage key chain of Elliott and E.T., a plastic version of the bike-flying-in-front-of-the-moon scene from the movie *E.T.* I've had this key chain since I was a little girl, and it's nearly impossible to lose because of its unnecessarily large size: approximately the dimensions of a small sandwich. And yet, on this occasion, while hanging out at a park with a friend, I lose the key chain.

I feel completely panicked. Mostly because I don't have a spare car key, but also because I've spent a long time being attached to the key chain. My friend and I look everywhere for the keys. We look on the playground, search the soccer fields, mine the parking lot. The thing is nowhere to be found.

I finally just stop in the middle of the parking lot and pray a desperate prayer: "God, please help me find my E.T. key chain. You know how much it means to me."

Eye roll all you want about coincidences and parking-spot prayers, and even silly, nostalgic attachments, but suddenly and dramatically, the key chain drops down my pant leg and crash-lands onto the asphalt in front of me.

Rationality says there must have been a hole in my pocket, where the key chain got stuck until the very moment I uttered, "Amen." But, decades later, I still wonder: Did God do that on purpose? Was that God's little game of hide-and-seek so that I would understand, years later, that God is the Finder of Lost Things?

☾

This year, fall has barely settled when Chicago winter, like a supervillain, sneaks in. While we are all delightfully distracted by pumpkin-spice lattes and apple-cider donuts, four o'clock in the afternoon starts to look and feel like midnight. It gets so cold that my boys have to wear winter gloves and scarves at the bus stop.

The sudden darkness and the unseasonably early brutal cold, alongside the spiritual dark night I am wading through, don't help my melancholy. It's honestly all very depressing. One afternoon, I've had enough and announce to my family, "I need magic and light and lovely Christmas décor, or I will not survive this winter. And you will not survive this winter if I can't survive this winter." So we pull out our Christmas tree a few weeks earlier than usual and begin sorting through our many boxes of decorations and ornaments.

What you need to know about our Christmas tree is that Kevin bought it off Craigslist from a shopping mall that was going out of business. It is three stories tall—basically the size of a California redwood tree. I was nursing a three-day-old baby—our youngest, Nolan—when Kevin and our other two sons burst through the door, proudly and wildly declaring, "Mom, guess what we found for you and the new baby! It's the BIGGEST TREE IN THE ENTIRE WORLD!"

As you can imagine, the Sampson Family Christmas Giant takes days to decorate. It's one of those all-hands-on-deck family traditions that my children now complain about but will surely treasure when they are older. And because of our tree's reputation around town, friends and neighbors regularly gift us with ornaments. Some of the ornaments are funny little gag-gifty things—a Swedish pickle or an ugly Santa. Some are sweet memories like the craft coffee-filter angels my sons made in kindergarten.

Other ornaments are in the categories of *special* and *fragile* and *expensive*, and I hang them high to avoid accidental dislodging. These ornaments hold nostalgia and memory from my childhood or Kevin's or from special trips throughout our marriage.

There's one ornament in this category that's not fragile or expensive or from my childhood treasury, but it is still very special. I was starting graduate school in Southern California years ago when I bought it. And at the time, I was battling insecurity and *not smart enough*–ness and, basically, felt very *unbrave* about the whole going-back-to-school thing.

So before starting class, I took myself to Disneyland alone—a place I'd adored as a little girl when I'd lived in Anaheim. I rode the same rides I'd ridden decades earlier and bought myself one of those ridiculous refillable plastic popcorn buckets to eat from while walking around the theme park. Somehow, as Adult Aubrey revisited Younger Aubrey, I found some newfound courage to begin the adventure of graduate school. Just before I left Disneyland, I purchased a little stuffed Robin Hood Christmas ornament as a reminder that I could do it. I could shoot my arrow and show up to something that seemed scary.

But this year, as we unpack our Christmas decorations and ornaments, I can't find Robin Hood. I sort through all our Christmas stuff more than once, but Robin Hood is nowhere to be found. I look online for a replacement, but of course it no longer exists. This afternoon, I spend *hours* alone in our dark attic, frantically throwing tissue paper everywhere, re-searching each storage tub I have previously sorted through. The stuffed Robin Hood ornament is simply *gone*, and I feel sort of pathetic and irrational for needing to find it so badly.

I decide, with disappointment, that some things are meant to be lost.

☽

This morning, before that frantic search through the attic, I tended to something else that has been lost.

I've been dreading today's breakfast meeting with an old friend. It's someone who moved away for a new job, and after she left, our friendship slowly died. I don't know who stopped texting, stopped replying, or stopped trying first. It was no one's fault, really. It was simply a matter of lost proximity. But at some point, with the distance on the map and the distance between touchpoints, the distance between *us* grew as well.

And in the middle of it all, Jenn was dying and I was in a dark night and I just didn't have capacity to do more than I was doing. There's this tragic truth about loss and hardship, something anyone who has grieved inevitably discovers, though that doesn't numb the sting—some friends can't, for one reason or another, go with you to the hard places. Some people can't handle the pain you carry. Some people aren't equipped for dark-night companionship. Some people simply can't be present, because life has changed.

This relationship, with all its distance and capacity struggles, had begun to feel fragile, like those ornaments. I have been angry about things, and she has been angry about things, and I would have probably avoided those conversations. To her credit, she wasn't willing to. She was in town for the holidays and asked me to meet.

Our breakfast started with small talk about Christmas decorations and holiday travel plans, and *Wow, isn't it sooo cold so early this year?* I ordered avocado toast and coffee and decided against ordering a side of bacon to sprinkle on the toast. Meanwhile, my friend didn't order any food. And when you don't order food at a breakfast place, that's a stand, isn't it? That's the quiet thing being said aloud. My heart started racing, and my pulse began thumping in my ears. This meeting would be more difficult than I had prepared for.

I glanced at the waitress several times for more coffee, hoping to have something warm to hold in my hands while I prepared to share my side of the story. But I soon realized this wasn't that. This conversation wouldn't be a give-and-take.

My friend needed to vent and be heard, and I was asked to listen. So I did. I regulated my breathing and pinched my thighs to stay present and contained my anger and loneliness and hurt, and I kept listening. And I believed her. I believed her hurt and her words, and I apologized for my part in it. I tried to be brave, and while I sat there, I was. But I cried the whole way home and forgot my leftover container of avocado toast on the table.

On that drive home from breakfast, I grew angrier and lonelier, and *that* energy is what drove me back to my attic for one more frantic search for my missing ornament. But it is gone, officially. And I need to let it go, just as I need to let so many lost things go.

•

In the book of Luke, Jesus tells three famous parables that are really just one long parable about lost-and-found things: a lost sheep, a lost coin, a lost son. As Jesus is telling these stories, what he's doing is asking and answering a question: *What is God like?*

God is a shepherd who goes after lost sheep.

God is a person who searches for lost treasures.

God is a welcoming father, running toward his lost children.

What is God like? Jesus insists that God is the Finder of Lost Things and Lost People and Lost Hopes and Lost Longings. And because Jesus is telling this story to the religious elite and to sinners as well, it is clear that on the spectrum of lost things, we can all be found—saints and sinners alike. But before something can be found, it begins as lost or becomes lost, whether that's a small token of nostalgia or the giant shadow of a relationship.

J. R. R. Tolkien once implied that because of Jesus everything sad will one day come untrue, and it will somehow be greater for having been broken.[1] I like to believe, similarly, that everything lost will be found again in Jesus. Or, as Frederick Buechner once said, "What's lost is nothing to what's found, and all the death that ever was, set next to life, would scarcely fill a cup."[2]

Sometimes it's necessary to say a gentle goodbye to things or dreams or people we love. It's hard and sad and bewildering but ultimately *good* to surrender back to God what doesn't want to be found. But other times, instead of goodbyes God gives us little hellos, little gifts of protestation against disconnection.

As I climb down from the attic, a car pulls into our driveway. It's a family friend who has watched my kids since she was a teenager. She yells to me from her car, "Hey! I was in the neighborhood. Need some help decorating?"

We spend the next couple of hours in the chilly winter air, hanging multicolored lights on the front-porch railings, covering the garden bed with white lights. By the time we finish, we are officially freezing, so we move inside, where I start a fire and make us some hot chocolate with gingerbread syrup. We warm up while laughing about her family's Christmas memories and traditions. We remember her brother, who died from cancer a few years earlier. We talk about Kevin's mom, who died a couple of years ago, and the other people and precious things we've lost along the way. She asks about Jenn.

Later, after my friend goes home, I clean up the mugs of hot chocolate, and the boys start decorating the mini Christmas trees they keep in their rooms. At some point during the evening, my youngest son thunders down the stairs, cheeks red, hair wild, smile massive.

"Mom! Guess what I just found!?!"

He is holding the Robin Hood ornament, triumphantly, found after being tucked away last year with his personal ornament collection.

☾

Some things are meant to be lost. It hurts, and it's hard. And sometimes God teaches us that our lost things are better left to his care.

But God is also the Finder of Lost Things. That means we can surrender our precious lost items and lost longings to God and trust that he will never chuck them carelessly into a dumpster. God never discards our concerns. God tucks them away in his journal for safekeeping until we are ready to have them returned to us. Or God sprinkles them throughout his garden to become something fragrant and new. Other times, God mends them, sews them up with shiny buttons and stronger threads, and creates a better fit overall.

Sometimes things are lost in the dark. But sometimes things wait to be found.

PART TWO

MIDNIGHT

God separated light from dark. . . .
He named the dark Night.

GENESIS 1:4-5, AUTHOR'S PARAPHRASE

You have taken from me friend and neighbor—
darkness is my closest friend.

PSALM 88:18

A LITURGY FOR DARKNESS AND GRIEF

O God.
God Who Sees in the Dark,
show us that you are here, sitting on our mourning benches with us.
Remind us that you hold our heads in your lap as we cry on the bathroom floor.
Teach us that you live at the bottom of our Kleenex box.
Oh, great God, be small.
Be tiny.
Be a miniature night-light in our hands.
A lamp would be overwhelming.
A light bulb too jarring.
But a tiny reading light, a thin sliver of light in our fingertips, even if we don't turn it on,
that's the right size for this dark hour.
There is a time for everything, and right now,
this midnight of our soul has some lessons to teach us.
So, God, we need you small and we need you near, but we also need you strong
because we cannot walk this dark path on our feet. We need to be held.
We reluctantly but willfully choose to surrender to whatever mystery you are inviting us into, in this darkest part of night.
But do not tarry.
Carry us through, to the other side of midnight.

6

THE LONGEST HOURS

Be Gentle with Yourself in Loss

Jenn cannot survive another winter.

She is in the ICU, and she keeps texting me, "I don't belong here." "I should be at home." "This is stupid." "I'm bustin' outta here."

But her oxygen level is at 45 percent, and her lungs aren't expelling carbon dioxide, and there's cancer in her lungs, heart, breasts, and lymph nodes. Jenn has delirium, tremors, and not much time left in the known universe.

Cancer is swallowing Jenn, and I am swallowing grief the weight of a thousand dying stars.

So tonight I am delivering food to Justin in the hospital—because bringing a hamburger and truffle fries to my dying best friend's husband, the father of her children, is the only thing to do. When our people are dying, we bring lots of food and lots of presents to their people.

In the hospital lobby, I hand Justin a gift basket for Jenn. It's filled with a soft, cream cashmere sweater, fuzzy socks, and a gnome mug that says, "cozy," because *cozy* is a necessity when cancer is winning. Losing a best friend is losing a thousand inside jokes and a thousand more instances of "I saw this thing at HomeGoods and it made me think of you."

Eventually, Justin will hand it all back to me—the basket, the socks, the mug. And I will wear the sweater nearly every day, nearly every morning with my coffee and my journal. I wear it now, as I type these words.

Where are you, God?

I need you to be small, be near.

Justin invites me to join him for dinner in the hospital cafeteria. His eyes are lined with red, and I watch as he picks at the truffle fries, scoots the burger from one side of the takeout container to the other. We take a picture together, and I text it to Jenn, who is lying in bed on a morphine drip in her hospital room just a few floors above us. I try to make her laugh by captioning the photo, "Look, I am on a dinner date with your husband."

She hearts the image and responds, "It's too intense here. Too many rules. I'm fine. I shouldn't be here. I don't even think this doctor is telling me the truth about things. Can you break me out?" I tell her that I'll shave my head and pretend to be her and she can put on a wig and sneak out as me.

Our days were filled with each other's voices. Author Joan Didion wrote something like that when her literary partner and husband died unexpectedly.[1] That is one of the truest things I can say about my best friend. We talk every day, throughout the day, on Voxer, over text, on voice text, on the phone, and in emails. We slide into each other's DMs, and, of course, we chat in real life, too. We have done so for twenty-plus years. And I can't make sense of not doing that anymore. Kevin said recently, "I miss hearing Jenn's voice throughout our house."

After not eating, Justin returns to Jenn, and I don't hear from either of them for hours, endless hours, tedious hours filled with so many questions. *How much time does she have? If she can get her oxygen levels back up, does that get her through Christmas? God, why now? God, why ever? God, where are you? God, can you please be small?*

Later that night, after Justin has gone home to tuck their three sweet sons into bed, kissing their foreheads and whispering lullabies over them, avoiding saying the Big Scary Thing to them yet, Kevin stops over to check on Justin.

"Don't tell Aubrey," Justin says, "but they are out of options. The doctor says it's too aggressive and there's nothing more they can do."

Kevin wants to say, "Aubrey already knows, friend," but he doesn't. Instead, he stays silent in that hallowed space, and the two of them stand there crying at the doorway of liminality, this in-between, this time of thinness, of waiting for death to welcome your person home.

Later, Kevin sneaks back over to Jenn and Justin's house after midnight to decorate it with Christmas lights. He wants Jenn to see her house lit up as she arrives home for hospice. If it's possible, I fall more in love with Kevin for this.

There's a Pulitzer Prize–winning play called *Wit* by Margaret Edson about an exacting English professor named Dr. Vivian Bearing who is dying of ovarian cancer, and ultimately, as most art is, it is also about love. A through line of the play is a long-standing literary debate over a sonnet by John Donne, "Death, be not proud." The conflict is around Donne's use of punctuation, whether he meant to use an exclamation point, a semicolon, or a comma at this line: "And death shall be no more, Death, thou shalt die."

Dr. Vivian Bearing's mentor, an openhearted, gracious scholar named E. M. Ashford, argues for the comma:

> This way, the *uncompromising* way, one learns something from this poem, wouldn't you say? Life, death. Soul, God. Past, present. Not insuperable barriers, not semicolons, just a comma.[2]

In the play, Ashford cares for Bearing while she is on hospice, steering away from academic wit and scholarly debate and choosing instead to read children's stories to her, stories about love and family and bunny rabbits.

Death is just a comma, not a period, for those in Jesus, and we are in that breath of a space before the comma as we wait for Jenn's prognosis. That space is very thin, but death is thinner still.[3] Death is not a wall. Death is not an exclamation point. Death is a doorway, a baptism, for those in Christ. Death, in Jesus, is the entrance to childlike, divine Love.

☽

Right now we're in Advent. Did I say that yet? I have lost track of time. If you have walked through fresh grief, you know what this is like, the time slippage. It could be Advent a decade ago. It could be Advent on Jupiter. It could not be Advent. I don't know, because I can't seem to make sense of ordinary time, let alone sacred time.

But I'm mostly sure it's Advent because as I am waiting for news of Jenn's time frame, Kevin keeps making me walk through our Advent rhythm, our homespun tradition. I don't totally appreciate what he is doing right now, making me stick to a schedule, a practice, a ritual. It's not because I don't want to appreciate it. It's mostly because I am entirely out of my body. I am floating, watching myself and my family practice our Advent ritual while my best friend is dying a few miles away. Yet I am grateful to Kevin because the pattern, the habit, keeps part of me anchored to the present and to my people while the rest of me is attached to a thousand balloons, floating over Delnor Hospital.

This is our Advent ritual: As soon as the dinner plates are cleared and the dishes are put away, the boys run around turning off every light in the house, even our Christmas-tree lights. Then we all gather back around our kitchen table in the full darkness. One of us, the chosen spokesperson for the evening, recites our DIY liturgy: "The world was in darkness. We were living in our sin. But God sent his Son, Jesus, to be . . ."

At this point, the spokesperson pauses and lights a match theatrically while the rest of us yell at the tops of our lungs, ". . . THE LIGHT OF THE WORLD!" We light a Christmas candle and then read part of the Christmas story from one of the Gospels.

I used to view this family tradition of ours as a grandstand against darkness, against evil. I saw it as a prophetic declaration that light will reign once more, that warmth will rise again. But I wonder, now, if we're not actually wishing away the darkness—because it's the darkness itself causing us to draw near. The darkness makes us lean in and listen, the way a hushed silence does. The same Advent ritual performed at noon would not be nearly as reverent. The darkness demands we pay attention.

There's a passage in Scripture, from Exodus, describing when God appeared to the Israelites in thick darkness. The people were terrified of God's presence, and they stood far away in fear. But Moses, the Bible tells us, "drew near to the thick darkness where God was" (Exodus 20:21, ESV). There are other places in Scripture where thick darkness is under God's feet, surrounding God like a canopy (e.g., 2 Samuel 22).

A good exegete might not read much into those moments, might not draw any theological conclusion about what it means that God, throughout history, has appeared in a confusing cloud of darkness. But right now, I don't need scholarship or wit. Right now, I am desperate to know that we can find God in the darkness as much as we can know him in the light.

For St. John and St. Teresa, the dark night of the soul was not sinister or evil but somehow good and even precious. As I think about my best friend, asleep in her ICU bed, the darkness covering her room, the hospital, I am not ready to call any of it good or precious, but I am still willing to look desperately for God here. So each night I walk through the family Advent tradition with my boys, and when it is over, I end up sitting alone at the kitchen table with the lit candle for a few minutes. I place my hand over my heart as I have done for so many months now. I remind myself that I am not slipping away into oblivion, and I pray, *O Light of the World, be here in the darkness. I need to know you are here. Be near my friend, too. Be her comma. Be her breath.*

•

If you are currently experiencing fresh grief, you know that as I write these words, I don't have much perspective to offer you. I am in it, too, wading through the longest hours of night. What I know is that it doesn't seem real and yet is the scariest thing ever. What I know is that you are being invited into depths you have yet to plumb, and that dive will require everything from you. The only thing I can think to say to you right now—because I keep saying it to myself—is *Be gentle with yourself.*

Say no to unnecessary commitments. You don't even have to give a reason. Just say no. Let people love you with meals. Take baths. Remember to wash your hair. Wear comfortable clothes. Take naps. Take walks. Remember to eat now and then. Buy yourself a soft stuffed animal to squeeze. The part of you that feels small when the world feels too big, too unbearable, will need some precious attention now. Let yourself receive it. And keep asking God to find you, or if you are too tired, stop asking and let friends take that role over for you . . . because there are days when grief will make you feel lost to yourself, to others, to God.

In these long, difficult, midnight hours of loss, you will grow weary. You will grow tired from pretending and pushing through and proving yourself and managing your pain. You will barely remember to shampoo, or even what shampoo is, and you will often not know what to do next. That's okay. Your only job right now is gentleness, self-compassion.

Part of the gentleness will feel very hard: to bring to mind, intentionally and often, that God is with you and working in this darkest moment. That because of Jesus, our inalterable assurance is that nothing—not cancer, not death, not anxiety, not fear, not grief, not heartache the size of the stars, not even the darkest of midnights—can separate you from the love of God

(Romans 8:38-39). This is easy to forget in early grief. It's not just easy to forget; it's impossible to believe and even more impossible to care about. But even if you don't remember it, it's true. Even if you don't feel it, it's true. Even if you don't believe it, it's true. If you do anything else right now in your grief, may you swallow that truth—that God hasn't abandoned you, because God loves you and will never stop loving you—alongside the hurt you are also being forced to swallow. (And I am so sorry for all you are being asked to swallow. Please, be gentle with yourself.)

Death, *taker* that it is, will try to steal so much from you. Death will rob you of your sleep, your peace, your appetite, your faith, your brain space, your capacity, your wherewithal, your rationality, your dreams. You are not broken. You are not doing anything wrong. You are grieving. Again, be gentle with yourself.

My friend Matt says,

> Being gentle requires that we be aware of the fragility of the world around us. That we pay attention to those we could harm (without intending to!) because we don't know about their particular vulnerabilities or issues.
>
> Gentleness also requires that we know ourselves well. We have to know what our own capacity is, what our strength is.[4]

Gentleness is certainly a softness, a grace. But it's also an awareness, a willingness to accept your own limits. Gentleness is taking your humanity seriously. If resilience is getting back up, gentleness is letting yourself lie down and rest.

I know you probably have people to care for and duties you can't ignore. But you also have permission to crumple up in a corner for a while and wrap a blanket around yourself. You are allowed to make mistakes. You can be as sad as you want to for as long as you want to, as angry as you want to for as long as you need to. These are the long, hard hours of darkness.

Other people might want you to make your pain potable for them because they haven't yet known grief so aren't comfortable with depth or heartache. They mean well. But you know better now. Because you are facing sadness, you know that to fake a brave face is a weak person's work. The heart may be a strong muscle, but it will crumble. The truly strong choose gentleness when their hearts are disintegrating to dust.

☾

There is a moment outside the ICU, just before I bring Justin his food and sit with him—a moment where the oncologist comes into Jenn's room to break a planet's worth of news to them. Justin texts, asking me to wait a few minutes outside so he can chat alone with the doctor.

I pull into a visitor parking spot but keep my car running, keep the heater blasting, a fight against the unflinching cold that feels fitting right now. I notice purple and pink Christmas lights, colors of royalty and bravery, decorating the trees outside the ICU.

There in that parking lot, in the Advent darkness, with twinkle lights dotting the trees in front of my best friend's hospital room, I pray Romans 8 over it all. I pray *no separation from God* over Jenn and Justin and their boys and over this strange moment in time, over all that is about to occur . . . or not occur.

Just then, my phone buzzes with a text.

"I don't know what this means," the texter writes, "but God has laid you heavy on my heart tonight. Wherever you are right now, I am in your corner, praying for you."

Even in the darkest night, even as we limp with exhaustion, the work of gentleness in the pain doesn't rest on us. Gentleness is a fruit of God's Spirit, which means God is always gentle.

Okay, God, you're here, I pray. *Your hand is reaching down into this dark night. Why you're moving the way you are, I'll never understand. Please be gentle with my friend, now and at the hour of her death.*

O great God, be gentle enough for us all.[5]

7

TOSSING AND TURNING

Wrestling with God When You Have No Strength

On my desk is a piece of spiral notebook paper that I can't seem to throw away. It's buried between two books, *To Bless the Space Between Us* by John O' Donohue and *Tell Me the Dream Again* by Tasha Jun. Written sloppily and hastily in black Sharpie, the note says,

- Trapped lung
- Boys don't know yet
- Palliative care
- Hospice
- Weeks

There was only one lie on the paper. The weeks were days.

)

Breast cancer is a victor, claiming territory in Jenn's lymph nodes, limbs, and lungs. She is in a wheelchair and breathing from an oxygen tank. Her heart is stopping, her lungs are filling with a hard and crushing fluid—it's called "trapped lung," apparently. When she leaves me messages these days, she pauses to cough, catch her breath, and try again. Most of her messages contain something like "Ehem. Ehem." Or "Hold on. I'll be right back; I need to gather my breath."

Jenn is being moved from the ICU to in-home hospice care tomorrow. Her second-born son, Hudson, who died nearly thirteen years ago, is waiting on tiptoe for his precious mama to come home to him.

God, where are you?

Right now, because life continues for me even though time is freezing for Jenn, I am writing a final paper for my postgraduate work, an Old Testament class. I'm writing about Proverbs 31, an acrostic poem that moves like an arrow to one point—a proverb within the proverb, the epilogue of the entire book of Proverbs: "Charm is deceptive, and beauty is fleeting; but a woman who fears the Lord is to be praised" (Proverbs 31:30).

The Proverbs 31 woman is called Woman of Valor, *Eshet Chayil.* She is a warrior woman who loves her people and has no fear of the future because she fears God.

So when Justin invites me to spend Jenn's last night in the ICU with her, I speak this over her: "You are a woman of valor, my friend. You are a Proverbs 31 warrior. You are Eshet Chayil."

To my surprise, Jenn replies almost defensively, "Well, if I am a warrior, so are you . . . so are all of us." She gestures to no one in particular. Then she adds thoughtfully, "What I mean is, you'll have to be brave, all of you will—to watch me dying, to say goodbye. You will have to be the warrior now."

While I am with her, Justin texts me, "Make sure she eats." So I pick up the hospital phone and order our last meal together, Jenn's last meal ever. Over twenty years of dinners out, girls' nights out, and sangria nights at our favorite tapas restaurant—over two decades of sitting under summer lights on back porches, over twenty years of sharing salads and appetizers, chili and fall soups—it all comes down to this, our final Communion from a hospital cafeteria: one Mixed Berry ICEE and a turkey sandwich. While I am on the phone ordering, Jenn whispers to me, conspiratorially, "Hey, Aubs, get the white bread. I'm finally splurging."

The food arrives, and I note that Jenn eats only one bite, takes only one sip. Her body is shutting down.

As we eat, she asks me hard questions.

She asks if she has done enough. "Have I lived enough for Jesus? Have I been faithful enough?"

"Did I miss the mark, Aubrey?" she asks me vulnerably, so vulnerably.

I put down my half of the sandwich and carefully climb into her hospital bed with her. I put my arms around her strange, changing, decreasing, skeletal body, and we both let ourselves weep and wail. We sing our songs of lament together, for all the things we have lost and are losing—for her kids, for her husband, for her family, and for our twenty-plus years of memories and moments and soul friendship. Then I gather my Eshet Chayil courage enough to say,

"Jenn, I have seen the Holy Spirit minister in you and through you for over two decades now. Jesus is in you. You are saved. You are good. You've done enough."

She replies with a sigh, "Thank you so much for saying that. I needed to hear that."

Then I say the most important thing I can say, "Plus, babe, there is no mark. Jesus bears the marks. There is no 'enough.' Jesus is enough. The Cross was enough."

And she responds, "Oh yes, that's right. Yes, thank you for saying that. I needed to hear that."

I continue, "And a good life is not about industry; it's about love. And Jenn, you have loved your people well. You have loved Jesus fiercely. You are a woman of valor, remember?"

At the same time, we start impromptu singing in falsetto, "WOMEN OF VALOOOORRRR," and then in this, our saddest moment, we burst into laughter. Because this is how our friendship works.

This is how our friendship worked.

•

I stay with Jenn in the ICU that night, hours after our last Communion together, where she asks me so many more questions.

"Aubrey, will I know Hudson? Will he know me?"

"Aubrey, will it be okay with estranged family I haven't talked to in years, the ones who are already there?"

"Aubrey, will it be peaceful?"

I say yes to everything. "Yes, you'll know Hudson. Yes, he'll know you. It will be perfect. Yes, you'll be fine with your family. It will be a grand reunion. Yes, it will be peaceful, not scary."

She says again, "Thank you for saying that. I needed to hear that."

It's not like I know any of these answers, really. But Jenn will know them soon.

☾

What is it about night that causes us to wrestle with God? Why does lying in bed at the end of a long day initiate an onslaught of worst-case scenarios, tomorrow's concerns, or thoughts about death? Why does nighttime act like a beacon for our anxieties, insecurities, and deepest apprehensions? Void of the day's distractions, to-do lists, and duties, night suddenly turns Pied Piper, summoning all the scary things near.

In Jenn's case, it's the raw vulnerability and reality of mortality. She's defenseless, left insecure and off-balance. Will the stories she has believed stand true? Will her faith have been enough? Will *she* be enough? This kind of grapple with God cannot occur when we are strong and secure. Only when we are exposed and enervated to the point that we can't *not* ask our hard questions, that's when they materialize. Night questions are lightning-rod questions, powerful enough to scorch the earth. But they are also baby-deer questions, clumsy fawns that wobble, tremble, and fall feebly to the ground.

When we think of wrestling with God at night, we typically look to the story of Jacob, the famed God grappler from Genesis 32. In my Bible, probably in yours as well, the subtitle of this story is "Jacob Wrestles with God." But that's not an entirely apt description. Because of the way the narrative unfolds, a more accurate subtitle would be something like "God Incites a Fight with Jacob."

Jacob was all alone by the Jabbok River. From there, the story's unfolding is vague and sudden. But what we pick up, right from the jump, is that Jacob didn't start the wrestling. God did. I can only use my imagination to fill in the missing details, but it almost reads like the God-man toed Jacob awake, provoking him. "Get up. You and me, kid. We're going to settle your past, your questions, and your relationship with me once and for all."

The wrestling is not actually told from Jacob's point of view. The God-man is the one who acts. Jacob is the one just having to respond.

- The man wrestled with Jacob (Genesis 32:24).
- The man saw that he could not overpower Jacob (Genesis 32:25).
- The man wrenched Jacob's hip (Genesis 32:25).
- Then the man said, "Let me go, for it is daybreak" (Genesis 32:26).
- The man initiated their post-battle conversation, inviting Jacob to reply (Genesis 32:26-29).

God wrestled.

God saw.

God wrenched Jacob's hip.

God said.

Truthfully, I don't understand this story, just like I don't understand Jenn's story unfolding in front of me. Most pastors who preach on this text say something like "Jacob was only able to wrestle God all night because God allowed him to. Obviously, God could have overpowered Jacob at any moment."

While that is true, maybe the point of this story is not about the fact that Jacob was able to wrestle with God all night. Maybe it's that God goaded Jacob into the match.

Because we think it's us, don't we? We think it's our doubts, our insecurities, our disillusionment. That's what leads to wrestling matches with God. But what if God *intentionally incites* us to doubt, to struggle, to question our faith? And what if God has a good reason for it?

There's a clue about this in the setting of Jacob's wrestling match: the Jabbok River. In the names Jabbok and Jacob, the *b* and *k* sounds are inverted, swapped, mirrored. Furthermore, Jabbok means "emptying." The storyteller of Genesis seems to imply that in the wrestling, God is emptying Jacob's false identity out of him. Jacob, who was known as *deceiver*, receives a new identity, a new name, on the other side of this restless night with God.

Here's what I think. I think all the bandages we mummy ourselves with in the night—our learnings, our achievements, our rigid beliefs, our certainty, our illusions of control, our proving our worth, our perfectly staged presentableness, all our posturing, even all our faux authenticity, all the ways we try to make ourselves acceptable, all the identity managing that we do—I think God grabs hold of a loose strand of that material and begins tugging on it. I think God unwinds and unwinds and unwinds with more and more urgency until we are suddenly tornadoing, spinning, unraveling. And when we have slowed down and the dizzying effect has worn off, we are left exposed, disclosed. We are as we were always meant to be with God, *naked and unashamed*. And it's right there—in the bottom layer, the underneath, the unveiled, unsheathed self—where the healing happens. Otherwise, the healing is shallow. And God is in the deep. All the way down, that's where God works. That's where God wrestles.

There's another wrestler in Scripture, a precursor to Jacob yet connected intimately to him. Jacob's beloved (if not *pained*) wife Rachel wrestled to have a child. Her sister, one of Jacob's wives (you know, 'cause patriarchy), was giving birth to son after son after son. All the while, Rachel remained childless and heartbroken. When Rachel's servant surrogate (again . . . patriarchy) finally gave birth to Jacob's sons, Rachel declared, "I have had a mighty struggle . . . and I have won" (Genesis 30:8, author's paraphrase). She named their second son Naphtali, which means "my wrestle."

Interestingly, in Rachel's mighty struggle, the Hebrew word translated "mighty" is *elohim*, the same word often used for "God."[1] Perhaps the Bible is saying, "Rachel wrestled with her sister and with God and prevailed, and she named her son Wrestle."

It's eerily similar to what the God-man says to Jacob after their battle: "Because you have wrestled with God and with humans and prevailed, you will be called Israel, 'he who wrestles with God'" (Genesis 32:28, author's paraphrase).

What do we learn from these similar stories? We learn that we *will* wrestle through the night as part of our faith journeys. That, though excruciating, the wrestling itself will reveal our true nature and will birth something new in us. And that God seems to incite it all. Again, God seems to very intentionally use the dark night. Maybe for our good. Most certainly for our transformation.

❯

For years, Jenn and I have passed a picture back and forth to one another. It's an inside joke, the picture. A wallet-sized glamour shot of a random woman, her hair and makeup done up like an

'80s supermodel. We don't remember how we got our hands on it, and I am sure she is a woman of valor in her own right, but the picture makes us laugh irreverently. If ever I see Jenn's car in the Target parking lot, I put it on her windshield wipers for her to find when she comes out of the store, and vice versa. One time I went to bed and it was literally *under my pillow*. The picture is this little secret exchange inside our friendship. So much of friendship is this, mundane inside jokes that cause full belly laughs.

We misplaced it for a while, the glamour shot, but recently while cleaning out her house, Jenn rediscovered it. That kind of cleaning should be for birthday parties and for guests arriving, but she was sorting through things so that no one would have to do it after she left, which is the saddest reason ever to clean.

Since she rediscovered the picture, we have passed the tiny photo back and forth in increasingly hilarious ways. Sometimes I imagine I'll stick it in her casket when no one is looking. But then I won't have it to remember, and I am greedy for all the tokens, all the memorials, all the keepsakes of my twenty-five years of best friendship. I want to braid Jenn into my hair and keep her there for the rest of my days.

In the classic children's book *Charlotte's Web*, as Charlotte the spider is dying, she says to Wilbur the pig, "You have been my friend. That in itself is a tremendous thing. I wove my webs for you because I liked you."[2]

My tremendous friend is about to die, so I weave some final webs for her. I make an appointment and get tattooed with the words *Eshet Chayil* in her handwriting. My warrior friend is braided in me forever.

And in my own wrestling match with God, these are the resolutions, the explanations, the answers I am desperate to wring out of him. *Why are you taking away my closest friend? Why are you stealing years of inside jokes and laughter? Why are you leaving me with nothing but tattoos and memories? Why, God, aren't you healing her? Why can't my precious friend wrestle a mighty wrestling with cancer and prevail?*

If I could be Jacob or Rachel for a night, meet God on the mat and pin him down, I would point my finger in his face or hammer my fists against his chest and demand some answers. I would scream a guttural "How could you?"

But I am drained from exertion. And I would only lose to a God who is much stronger than me. God would inevitably remind me that one touch of his fingertip could make me limp the rest of my life. God would likely tell me he created the stars, the sun, the moon, and the midnights. I, on the other hand, did not. I cannot.

There is a tender part of me, though, the underneath part, that longs for God, in our wrestling, to delicately grab my wrists and pull me in close, hug me tightly, and quiet my spirit. I want God to brush assurances of comfort over the top of my head and whisper soothing lullabies over my soul. This is close to something my friend Jenn is saying now, as she faces the end of her days—the end of her wrestling: "I may never be healed. But I will be held. And that's enough."

I want to be held.

Maybe this is the point of wrestling with God in the shadows. It is not about winning or losing; it's about proximity. We have to draw near and stay close in order to brawl.

I just wish the wrestling didn't feel so much like wilting.

I wish we walked away with a swagger instead of a wound.

8

SHIFTING SHADOWS

Facing Spiritual Disillusionment

Last year, at our church's staff Christmas party, we pushed several long plastic tables together to make one giant rectangle. At that table of tables, we went around, taking turns, saying words of affirmation over each person there. We started with Justin. We ended with Jenn. As that happened, an intrusive, unbidden thought settled in the front of my brain: *Jenn will not be here next year. She will not be here next Christmas.*

This thought has haunted me for nearly a year now. I have kept it a secret, wondering if I heard the voice correctly. I have wondered if it was God or fear or something evil from the spiritual realm. But I think I knew all along it was God. It was the Spirit whispering to me, preparing me. I recognized the voice like I'd know my own if I time traveled to the future to meet older me or time traveled to the past to meet younger me; I knew with a bewildering recognition.

I don't know if you are from a faith tradition that believes we can receive "words from God." I did not grow up with that kind of church experience—but I believe God speaks to his children. God has spoken to me through impressions, phrases, verses, visions, words, creation, and other people over the years, as I am sure God has also spoken to you.

But this word at this table?

This is the moment when the dark night of the soul becomes an unbearable burden. When God's obscurity becomes something else. Spiritual disillusionment, maybe? An encumbrance, perhaps?

St. John, in his medieval, Trinitarian style of explaining things, breaks the dark night of the soul into two phases. *The dark night of the soul* covers it all, an umbrella of sorts. Huddled under the umbrella are *the dark night of the senses* and something darker, *the dark night of the spirit.*[1]

The dark night of the senses is the obscurity of dusk, the sense that God's presence is hidden, hazy. When we sense God's absence, it is painful and frustrating but confusing in such a way that we still feel confident God is with us in the dark. This is what most of us walk through when we experience a dark night of the soul. The dark night of the spirit is a much deeper darkness. It's not always linear, and it's not always certain to occur. But when it does, a night faith feels insufficient. When the dark night becomes spiritual midnight, doubt is all around us, and we feel wholly lost.

Maybe you know what this is like. Because of the loss you are facing, the pain you are carrying, the fear and confusion about what God is or isn't doing, you feel like you are careening toward *something*, though you don't quite know where you will land. What you *do* know is that something is beginning to feel a lot like hopelessness, like desperation.

If the word I heard from God at that Christmas party was true—that Jenn would die a year later—then God knew Jenn would die. And of course God knew. God knows all. But that also means that over the past year, as I prayed, begged, screamed, and fasted for God to intervene and heal Jenn, God would not. God did not.

Why would God tell me that the worst was coming? Why would God know and do nothing?

Though I can't name the exact moment, it was somewhere in the midst of this—in the middle of coping with the reality of Jenn's impending death and beating my head against so many unanswered questions—when my dark night began to darken to midnight. This is when I began to join in with the chorus of the prophet Jeremiah's cries:

> He has made me dwell in darkness
> like those long dead.
>
> He has walled me in so I cannot escape;
> he has weighed me down with chains.
> Even when I call out or cry for help,
> he shuts out my prayer.
>
> LAMENTATIONS 3:6-8

I have prayed for cancer eradication and miracles and healing and wholeness, but it is clear now: The still, small voice in my head was true. Jenn will die soon, so very soon.

•

St. John of the Cross and St. Teresa of Ávila described the dark night as mysterious and obscure but still used affectionate phrases to describe the experience. They characterized the dark night in terms of God's love and the soul's happiness. There is another kind of darkness, though, what Teresa referred to as *tinieblas*—a wretched part of midnight, the darkest night of the spirit. This is not the oscura night of Teresa and John. This is something else entirely. Psychiatrist and theologian Dr. Gerald May explains,

> There is no doubt about the difference. Teresa uses *oscura* in saying that the spiritual life is so dark she needs much patience. . . . But she uses *tinieblas* when she says, "The devil is darkness itself." . . . In *oscuras* things are hidden; in *tinieblas* one is blind. In fact, it is the very blindness of *tinieblas*, our slavery to attachment and delusion, that the dark night of the soul is working to heal.[2]

Attachment and delusion: The darkest part of night shifts its shadows toward both, pointing ethereal fingers in their direction so we'll pay attention. This is another mystery of the dark night—this process feels so utterly painful, yet God elucidates our delusions and attachments not so that we'll be condemned. So that we'll be freed.

What are attachments? *Any thing, any person, any habit we use to numb or avoid pain.* What are delusions? *Any false ideas we have about God and life, including our ability to control God or God's presence.* The two are intertwined. What we believe about God leads the way to our attachments. If God is withholding, rigid, disappointed, untrustworthy, quick to shame or judge or punish you when you fail or doubt or stumble, then obviously you would run in any other direction to cope with pain. Of course you would seek out distractions and soothing from anything *but God.*

But if God is *for* you? If God is with you and comforting you and saving you and sanctifying you and convicting you without condemning you and loving you all the while, then any other attachment would itself become an illusion, would be seen as the mirage it really is. Spiritual dark nights tend to usher all the distorted views we have about God and ourselves to the forefront of our hearts so that we can begin wrestling with them, facing them, healing from them.

But.

The tinieblas night can also lead to something else—spiritual disillusionment, the feeling of being disappointed with God after discovering a new truth about God or after an experience that upsets your previously held beliefs. Bringing to mind the old adage *Never meet your heroes,* spiritual disillusionment leads to shaking your head with cynicism at God. *You are not who I thought you were.*

You are not alone if this is your experience of God at midnight. When faith suddenly feels thin and easily ruptured like a thin layer of soap across the water, then of course you will be left a little frail yourself.

☾

When Jenn goes on home hospice, Justin lets me come in and out to be with her in her final hours. I'll never stop being grateful to him for that. Justin calls me one night, in the middle of the night, whispering that Jenn is experiencing scary hallucinations and has no sense of peace or comfort from God. It feels like the tinieblas night, and Justin confesses that he is not doing okay watching it all happen.

In the darkness of my bedroom, I swear and scream at evil to get away from Jenn, from them all.

I drive to their house the next morning, very early, and pray over Jenn, "God, you don't promise us a happy ending, but you do promise you'll be with us in the valley of the shadow of death. Be true to your promises now. We beg you to be true to your promises now." I pray that her going would be sheltered and her welcome assured.[3]

In my lowest days in grief, which will come very soon—when I can't get off the couch and when I wonder if God is real, when the darkness blocks all I can see—I will consider that it is a treacherous thing to hear bad news from the God of goodness, the God of love. I hated that I knew for almost a year that Jenn would die before Christmas this year. But I will also remember that I heard God, specifically and accurately, and that means that God is real and God speaks to his children. I will also remember that after I prayed over her that morning, Jenn could finally sleep; she had peace. God was there, comforting her, because God is here in the dark of midnight, overcoming the tinieblas.

There is not much else to say about this now. I am in the thick of sadness, the throes of disappointment, and I don't have enough distance from grief to offer a clear vantage point on it. Perhaps this one thing: I have to believe that waking up from our delusions is good.

Because to live with illusions is to exist in falsehood about God, yourself, and others. To be free from spiritual illusions (to be *dis*-illusioned) means we can finally walk in reality. I think about the apostle Paul's first encounter with Jesus, described in Acts 9. God blinded the apostle so that he could learn to truly see. Then he healed his blindness so that he could live free. There is a blindness God heals and a blindness God brings *in order to* heal. The latter is the dark night.

I cannot control God. I cannot change what is fixed. I cannot stop death. I cannot numb enough or run far enough to escape the pain of loss. I don't know how to take a step forward in my spiritual midnight. I don't know how to say goodbye to my best friend. I don't know how to wrestle my way out of my disenchantment with God. But I am beginning to think that in accepting these tender realities, we pull down a star or two from the night sky, crush them in our hands, and sprinkle them across our darkened paths. *Please let there be star crumbs at my feet when I look for them. Please let them guide my friend home in peace.*

Somewhere beneath the back of my throat, all the way down my sternum, at the center of my chest, blinks a barely audible message. *God is not flimsy. God is not a soap bubble.*

My soul remembers this, even if my grief does not.

9

HOLDING ON IN THE DARK

What Tethers Us to God at Midnight

I can't sleep for crying. Can't go to UPS without sobbing. I wear sunglasses in Walgreens because my eyes are puffy and my nose is red. I look like I am sick, but I am heartsick, which is something else entirely.

In our dark-night journey, we've reached the middle of the night. This is when the grief is so raw, so intense, so fresh—when there is no light at all, not even reflecting off the moon's surface, and it's hard to know if the sorrow will ever lift. We're walking around in a daze of fatigue and formlessness. This is when our path through the night gets confused, chaotic, twisted. This is when we start tripping, stumbling, maybe even crawling our way through, scraping our knees and palms because we can't see how rocky the terrain is. Or we just lie down to nap because we are so spent. Getting through no longer feels like the point. Holding on in the dark is plenty.

Only a few months ago, I was confidently placing my hand on my heart and reminding myself that I am contained, not spilling out everywhere. But now there is only slippage, only spillage. My limbs and lungs and guts and organs have untethered themselves from my body and are floating away, a dozen strange rafts adrift on a black sea of ambiguity.

I am undone. I am Peter sinking in the waters of doubt. I need Jesus' hand to reach down, lift me out, and tie all my disparate pieces back together. But how can I hold on to Jesus' hand when I'm losing my grip? How can any of us stay connected to God in the darkest hours of midnight?

☽

What keeps us tethered to God at midnight? Lament.

I viscerally feel the words of pastor-poet Grace P. Cho:

> Show me
> How to wail and whimper
> Weep and scream
> The anguish
> Through guttural cries
> Teach me the rhythm
> Of pounding my chest
> And loosen my lips
> To sing the notes of lament.[1]

I keenly understand the words of the weeping prophet-poet Jeremiah:

> My eyes fail from weeping,
>   I am in torment within;
> my heart is poured out on the ground
>   because my people are destroyed.
>
> LAMENTATIONS 2:11

Thus far, my midnight of the soul has felt like a mash-up of confused genres—rooms in an eclectic museum that cannot quite decide on its theme. One room is topography, mountains and valleys. Another, a horror show. The next is a bizarre Easter-egg hunt, with so many things lost and found. From there, we make our way to the severe-weather pattern room—threatening and dangerous. I have not been a willing explorer; the dark has pulled and pressured me through every corridor.

And to be brutally honest, I don't even know how to pray my way through this befuddling night museum, because half the time it seems like God isn't listening. The other half, he's telling me things I don't want to hear. So my lips are loosened. I am in it. I am pounding my chest with lament's rhythm. My eyes are weak from weeping because my friend is being destroyed.

When we can no longer find the words or the wherewithal to pray, tears are a prayer. Pain is a prayer. Mourning is a prayer. Groans and sighs are prayers. Screams are a prayer. Punching walls is a prayer.

Cry in the shower. Demand answers. Scorch the earth with your grief and your anger. This is a strange gift at midnight, that we have a God who wants to hear and hold our anguished questions, our confusion, and even our rage.

•

What keeps us tethered to God at midnight? Trusted friendship. Safe community.

My friend Hollie and I cry on the phone. We make guesses about Jenn's time frame. We wonder what's next. But then, because we can't control any of this, we just cry some more. Hollie flies in from Seattle so we can, at the very least, weep together in person, so she can say her own goodbye to Jenn. So she can tend to me. So we can tend to each other. I don't know how any of us would persevere through suffering without friendship. Friendship is survival.

We all, our friends in this small grieving circle, reassure ourselves, "Well, at least she won't be struggling much longer," and we're thankful for that. But I wonder if that's totally honest. I don't want her here struggling any longer, but I want her here longer. Jenn is my person, the person I want to call and process this with, whose advice I need to handle it. I don't know how to get through Jenn's dying without Jenn's support.

Hollie is staying at my house now and she keeps wrapping me in blankets and feeding me hot chocolate with the "good, Oberweis milk, not the cheap stuff." She makes me eat buttered popcorn and watch Hallmark Christmas movies until she has to fly back to Seattle. Before she leaves for O'Hare airport, she pops me one last tub of popcorn, turns on my Christmas lights, lights some of my holiday candles, and shows me funny pictures to make me laugh. She reminds me to get some rest. Her visit was a blur. She basically hosted me. I was her guest in my house. While carrying her own grief, she was reminding me, with all that popcorn and hot chocolate, that we are not alone.

Trusted friendship; safe community. These will keep you connected to God and to yourself when you feel like you are fading away or falling apart. You will be tempted to isolate when you're wrapped in grief. Or the opposite may happen: You will become so unexpectedly vulnerable that you will unknowingly let unsafe people in. Grief can become desperation, exhaustion, a state in which it becomes too difficult to not let yourself be carried, and so you may inadvertently let your guard down and somehow allow well-meaning but unhealthy people to get too close. Just because they want to fix you and care for you doesn't make them the right people for the job.

But proven people, safe people—those are the ones who have been there all along, who have shown that they don't need you to soothe their wounds by being there for you in yours. They don't make your grief about themselves.

In your darkest moments, let the proven people love you and feed you and turn on lights for you. This is God showing up in the dark.

☾

What keeps us tethered to God at midnight? Moments of goodness amid all the hard.

Noticing goodness in the world when your soul is in lunar eclipse might seem trivial or cliché. But psychologist and Holocaust survivor Viktor Frankl says, "Suffering ceases to be suffering at the moment it finds a meaning."[2]

The author of Ecclesiastes wrote something not dissimilar: "The heart of the wise is in the house of mourning" (Ecclesiastes 7:4).

There is a hard-won, holy wisdom and meaning that can only be learned in pain and suffering. And while "wisdom" and "meaning" might feel like weak consolation prizes when weighed against the size and scale of your losses, what keeps the soul connected to God in heartache is that very notion: that meaning can be made, that gladness can be found, even in the darkest places.

So tonight I am keeping watch for goodness. My son Lincoln has a middle-school orchestra concert featuring a Christmas medley, and he's been working very hard on the viola to master these holiday songs. I want to stay home and hide forever. But I want to show up for my son more. So I must pause my crying. Let my eyeballs dry out a bit. Wash my face and put on my courage. I don't bother applying makeup, because even though I am willing myself to pause my tears for the moment, I will inevitably just cry it all off anyway. But I want to cheer on Lincoln. Jenn would want me to cheer on Lincoln. So we all—me, Kevin, and our other two sons, wrapped in our winter coats and winter concerns—attend this winter event.

We are a little late, due to my failed attempts at not crying, and the theater is packed. We are ushered upstairs to a tiny balcony, which is actually quite lovely because it is empty, save for a few other late arrivers, and we can see the whole stage below. A Christmas tree on stage right, five giant poinsettia plants at center stage, and Lincoln, stage left, playing "Silent Night" and "Joy to the World."

In my grief fog, I must have forgotten to help Linc pick out an outfit for the concert. The other orchestra members have donned ugly Christmas sweaters and elf hats, and Lincoln is in jeans and his dad's oversized hoodie. Still, he plays his heart out, I like to think, in his Auntie Jenn's honor.

He loves the songs he is playing tonight, and there is unapologetic joy on his face. He's also in that absolutely iconic middle-school stage where he's trying to grow his hair out, but his bangs keep falling in his eyes, and he keeps trying to shake the bangs out of his eyes, and he can't quite do it because of the whole playing-the-viola thing. So Linc spends the entire concert waving his hair around like a cool pop star. It's a little early–Justin Bieberish, which Jenn would have loved and laughed with me about.

And honestly—between Lincoln's hair flipping and this entire group of middle schoolers playing off-key while wearing Santa hats and the parents clapping along, their faces filled with pride, videoing the entire shindig on their phones for grandmas and grandpas and the Christmas trees and the poinsettias and the Christmas lights strung over it all—this room is overflowing with delight and vitality and spirit. There is so much love in this theater.

I am noticing that love, drawn in by it, when my oldest son leans over and whispers urgently, "Mom, this is so boring—when will it be over?"

I put my hand on his knee and whisper back, "This is the good stuff of life, buddy. Don't wish it away. These moments are not forever."

☽

Jenn dies just a few days later, on the winter solstice, the darkest day of the year. For the past two years, in solidarity with Jenn, those of us on her support team have all donned camo clothing on Wednesdays, her chemo day. We have posted pics and called it #warriorwednesday. And when Jenn's final breath becomes air, it is, somehow fittingly, somehow graciously, on a Wednesday night. Sometimes we wonder, *God, where are you?* Other times, God makes it so obvious.

I feel it, in my bones, that she is leaving. I fall on my bedroom floor and sob—my prayer of release. Then, after many nights of not sleeping while she was on hospice, I sleep like I am hibernating. I sleep because I can no longer change the thing I most want to.

I was with her that morning before she passed. She told me she loved me, drool dripping out of her mouth, just one more indignity as death drew near. I wiped it with Kleenex and told her I loved her, too. She would have hated being seen like that by others, but not by me. I got to see her in all her states, and I am thankful for people who say, "Yes, you are safe enough to let me be vulnerable with you." Even in her final hours, she and I were safe for each other.

In the end, Justin promises me, she went peacefully, no fear in her eyes.

Jenn has been welcomed home to her son Hudson, reunited with him in the realm of no cancer, no coffins, no disconnection. But the ones who love her, all of us who are trying to somehow stay upright in the dark, are left to wait.

We—you and I—are left to grieve and to wait. We are, all of us, just trying to hold on in the dark. Theologian Fleming Rutledge says, "The church lives between two advents. Jesus Christ has come; Jesus Christ will come." And "If you find this tension almost unbearable at times, then you understand the Christian life."[3]

So yes, it is dark and lonely and cold and unbearable, and we are in waiting. For those of us who know Jesus, we wait with hope. We do. Those hands will reach down and stop us from sinking. They will. They have to.

What keeps us tethered to God at midnight? Jesus.

Still, some separations cause a shocking and formidable sadness. The only thing to do, in the lingering in-between, is this:

Play our notes of lament.

Love and be loved by the ones who are safe, the ones who dare to come close and hold grief space with us.

Keep watch for moments of goodness and love to slice through the darkness.

And the most confounding: Let Jesus do whatever Jesus does in the darkest of hours.

It will take a very, very long time before we see what Jesus does at midnight. But I know this now: It has something to do with reintegrating (maybe even remaking) all that has split apart.

10

A STRANGE NEW ORBIT

Letting Go When Nothing Makes Sense

I go to Starbucks and Dunkin' the morning after Jenn dies to bring Justin and his boys some food, which is an entirely normal thing to say now. *The day after my best friend died, I went to get her husband and sons some food.* I went to get her widower husband and motherless children some breakfast.

Food won't glue anyone together, but it's a type of shelter. My oldest son, Eli, recently got a job washing dishes at a local coffee shop, and yesterday he rode his bike to the dollar store, used his dishwashing money, and purchased sixty-one dollars' worth of candy. Then he dropped it off for Jenn's sons. *Here, this sugar is an offering of love. Here, this gargantuan bag of candy is a way for you to make it through the next ten minutes.*

I don't like that her death is a calendared item because it makes no sense that time moves on, carelessly carrying us with it. I am certainly not choosing to move the clock forward while my best friend is frozen on a date behind me. No, not frozen. Just gone. What is death? Goneness.

Both places, Dunkin' and Starbucks, feel so ordinary. The drive-through lady at Dunkin' can't understand me through the intercom. "No, I don't want a Box O' Joe, I want a box of Munchkins. Not coffee, just the donuts" is the most mundane exchange in the entire universe. But I am so aware that it's happening. *The most conventional conversation in the most average suburb of Chicago is happening right now.* That's what I keep thinking.

At Starbucks, the barista accidentally makes an extra vanilla latte and asks if I want it. I start sobbing—I suppose because of the kindness of a free latte. "I am not fit for public consumption right now," I bumble, running out the door, embarrassed by my messiness. Again, there's that awareness: *I was just crying in Starbucks, where everyone around me is just there for coffee and breakfast sandwiches.*

A couple of nights later, on Christmas Eve—*How in the world is it Christmas Eve after Jenn has died? What is time?*—Kevin and I take our boys to a holiday movie to try to offer them some Christmas normalcy. Throughout the film, I keep thinking, *Going to the movies is the most normal thing in the world. But how many people in this theater lost their best friend two days ago? What are the statistics of that? What does the data tell us?* Everyone at the movies just buys popcorn and Twizzlers, and they leave to go to the bathroom and then return, and it's all so commonplace. But for me, the whole time I am doing these things, I am *noting* them. I am so very aware of the fact that *I am at the movies now*. I used to just go to the movies. Now I am conscious that I am going to the movies.

People around me keep saying, "Don't feel guilty for living your life and enjoying your family at Christmas." I don't. I don't feel guilty for enjoying the life that is in front of me. Jenn would want me to celebrate and live. But I am just *so very aware* of the moments of enjoying. It's like these particular clothes are too peculiar, hanging awkwardly off my shoulders. The sleeves are too long, too gangly. So no, I don't feel guilty. I feel cognizant. Is this what it means to have an out-of-body experience? I don't know. All I know is that death has made me acutely and awkwardly aware of the normalcy of life.

The thing about death is that there is nothing to understand. Death is vacuous. It's privation. It's void. It's gap. It's total uninhabited space. That's not something one can comprehend, not something humans can make sense of. How can anyone understand *absence*? Poet Edna St. Vincent Millay once wrote to a friend, "The presence of that absence is everywhere."[1] That's the wild thing about nonexistence; it exists all around us.

The villain of the 1984 fantasy film *The NeverEnding Story* is called "The Nothing," a dark force sweeping the magical land of Fantasia. The aptly named Nothing erases everything in its path until the young narrator and hero, Bastian—a boy grieving his mom—yells his mother's name into the universe. The Nothing's reign of terror is over.

I have sat with Jenn's three sons lately, playing cards, doing laundry, laughing and crying with them. When they leave my house, or when I leave their house, I inevitably end up thinking of them as Bastians, just needing to yell their mom's name to stop The Nothing that is death from overcoming them. That's too much sadness for a son, for any little one, to carry.

Bastians should not have to be the ones to stop The Nothing. The Nothing should never have come. But that's death. Death is a Nothing that just keeps coming.

And yet.

Jesus' name stops The Nothing because death is dead in Jesus. And I am straining with every faith muscle, every spiritual nerve ending, to hold fast to that truth right now, because I am telling you, loss and grief and the dark night are good at making us forgetful. When I don't know what else to do, when my own faith muscles feel incapable of holding up this heavy weight, I borrow the faith of grievers before me. I return to the lamenters of Psalm 88. I keep crying out with their words:

> You have taken from me my closest friends.
>
> PSALM 88:8

> My eyes are dim with grief.
>
> PSALM 88:9

> I call to you, LORD, every day;
> I spread out my hands to you.
>
> PSALM 88:9

> Are your wonders known in the place of darkness,
> or your righteous deeds in the land of oblivion?
>
> PSALM 88:12

But I cry to you for help, LORD;
    in the morning my prayer comes before you.
Why, LORD, do you reject me
    and hide your face from me?
PSALM 88:13-14

You have taken from me friend and neighbor—
    darkness is my closest friend.
PSALM 88:18

God has taken from me my best friend and neighbor. Darkness is my companion. Divine absence is my comrade. Nothingness is my colleague. And I am not doing okay with the emptiness of it all.

•

For the past few nights, I have dreamt about Jenn. If you have known early grief yourself, you also know that it brings a slew of strange, vivid dreams. Last night I was the manager of some massive hotel. I wore an apron, then a business suit. Sometimes I was holding Jenn's babies. At one point, I was holding all these babies, asking them what I should say at their mom's funeral. "Don't mention video games," the babies said. "She wouldn't want that."

In my dream, I kept searching the hotel grounds for her. Jenn would be in one room. I'd go to find her, only to discover she had just left that room. I caught a glimpse of her long, blonde hair leaving a room at one point, but I kept getting there too late. I kept missing her.

I keep missing her.

Because I don't know what to do with all this nothingness and normalcy, with all these disorienting, nonsensical dreams, I just *keep* keeping myself busy. My errands become a little manic, honestly: I drive from Starbucks and Dunkin' to Target and Walgreens to Costco and T.J. Maxx. I am frantically running errands to be helpful and, honestly, to avoid my pain. Keep moving. Keep the motor on. Don't stop. Just keep driving. Just keep running.

When we lose our people, the relationships don't just evaporate. Our twenty-five years of "Jonathan and David" friendship, as someone recently called it, doesn't die just because Jenn did. And all that kinetic momentum doesn't just dissipate; it demands to go *somewhere*. Grief, as others have said, is *love with nowhere to land.* Or what's that famous line from *WandaVision*? "What is grief, if not love persevering?"[2]

> What is grief, if not *love abruptly interrupted*?
> What is grief, if not *love's collision with an invisible, impervious boundary*?
> What is grief, if not *looking for Jesus to make something from the Nothing that is death*?
> What is grief, if not *frantically running errands, hoping it will bring back your person*?

While driving back and forth from one to-do to the next, I'm listening to things in a blur, avoiding pain with noise as much as with tasks. Between podcasts and radio shows and YouTube videos and audiobooks, everything runs together. In the mess of white noise, I hear someone, or several people maybe, say some version of "It's important to dig deep wells in your grief. In your heartache, fill yourself up. Soak life in so that you become a deep-water body of wisdom." This voice, or these voices—I don't really know because grief brain is soup brain—suggest the griever fill up his or her days with literature, art, music, study, travel, experiences, rich creativity, and adventures. And I get it, I guess. That's a good formula for developing a deep-well kind of life, but it's terribly tone-deaf advice in early grief. Digging deep wells requires the tools and the strength to jab and shovel the earth. And in this frantic, upside-down reality of fresh grief, it's hard to do much more than lie down next to a puddle.

When you're falling to the ground in tears every few hours or running around like the proverbial chicken with no head, your only job is to exist. Someday you'll have capacity for "soaking life in." But now is not the time to feel any pressure or shame to do more than you can. With every ounce of strength I can muster (which is admittedly not many ounces), I give you permission, in your early days of grief, *not* to dig any wells.

Recovery is slow work. It takes a long time.

I have said this before, but it bears repeating: You can feel what you need to for as long as you need to. Period. Done.

But, paradoxically, something else is true: Even as we can do nothing but exist—*endure*—in the absurdity and surreal normalcy, in the intrusive pain and seemingly endless tears, we are somehow *becoming* a deep well. Whether or not we want to. Whether we do anything creative or meaningful. Whether all we can do is breathe, drink some water, and sit on the couch in a daze. Or whether we stumble through Target like a madwoman on a mission.

What I am trying to say is this: Whatever you are capable of (or incapable of) in your fresh pain, you have permission to just *be*. You even have permission to change your mind throughout the days—throughout the minutes—about the best way to be. In fact, *not knowing what to do* is a perfectly reasonable way to survive the initial onslaught of grief.

And maybe that's how it actually happens: You become a deep well in early loss *not* by digging or cultivating or filling up your days with art and adventure but by dealing in a whole lot of *I don't knows*. By giving yourself permission to simply be, bit by bit, grace by grace—that is how you will develop the depth and fortitude necessary to move through heartache.

For me, I don't know if I should keep driving from place to place, from one errand to the next, or stop running and try on stillness for a bit. I feel like I've become a flotation device, detached from my body, blowing and bouncing around aimlessly. So maybe slowing down, getting still, would allow the voice of loss to speak its pain and help my healing. Maybe it would anchor me. Admittedly, I don't quite know how to pause my internal engine long enough to tend to my needs. And I don't really want to, not yet anyway. That's okay. That can't be forced either. Those days will come. Today, I permit myself to be. That's all I can do anyway.

Grief launches us on a strange new orbit, and for now, we're getting our bearings while the earth reels in an entirely different direction than we're used to. So let's let grief take us wherever it needs to, and let's not feel shamed or pressured to do or be anything else. I'll try if you try. Or I'll change my mind about trying. That's okay too.

I will tell you this. One place my early grief eventually takes me is a small, aching, defiant act. It won't feel important or *deep well*–ish to anyone. But it's a tiny, and in my mind important, way to pause and honor my pain and sadness:

> Soon it will be time to pack up the Christmas decorations for the year, hauling them back into their storage space in the attic.
>
> As I do, I will think, *Jenn was here, in the world, when we unwrapped these. She's not here now.*

Such a noteworthy demarcation, such a notch in the universe's timeline. Every Christmas from now on, Jenn will not be in the world. This makes no sense to me, the way death makes no sense.

> But I will leave out one winter twig of decorative greenery anyway.
>
> I will wrap it in twinkle lights and set it by a framed photo of Jenn and me.

It's not literature or theology or a richly creative notion. It's not adventure. But it serves as a tiny, little breath blowing against The Nothingness. It is Christmas persevering.

Now more than ever, in the nothing and normalcy of death, I need something small enough not to feel like pressure but possible enough to stand as a vigil.

11

THE STILL OF THE NIGHT

How the Soul Expands in Grief

We hold Jenn's funeral—well, her "celebration of life"—near the end of Christmastide. It is on a Wednesday. A final Warrior Wednesday. Kevin leads parts of the service. I give her eulogy. It's a blur.

It is funny, though, the things that strike you in these moments. The whole time I am speaking, I just keep thinking about my left arm.

During my words of remembrance for my best friend, my left arm just lies there, lifeless on the podium like a dead fish. I speak on platforms regularly. When I speak publicly, I might use the podium or stand as a place to keep my notes, but I never stay behind the podium reading. I never stay static on stage. I literally work the stage. I walk. I move. I glide, even.

For Jenn's service, I can't do any of it. My legs are shaking, and I can barely lift my head to look at the audience. And that arm—my weird left arm is just there, frozen in time and space. My arms and legs are staying in one place, but my nose is running. I don't have enough Kleenex for my teary eyes and runny nose. While reciting my speech, I keep thinking, *I should have brought more tissue up here. Can't anyone see that? Why isn't someone bringing me a tissue?* But they all have their own tissues that aren't enough.

The whole time I keep thinking, *Is this weird that my arm is here? I don't normally put my arm here on a podium like this. This posture is unnatural.* This whole day is unnatural.

Jenn and I talked about her funeral before she died. She wanted me to hide a prize under someone's chair and have them find it during the funeral, like a Big! Surprise! Giveaway! at a carnival. She also wanted to me text everyone from her phone at the end of the service: *Thank you for coming.* I don't do either of these things, but I tell the stories, and everyone laughs at her dark sense of humor. She also told me to tell everyone about Jesus: "Just make sure you tell people about Jesus, or none of it was worth it."

So I tell them about Jenn and Jesus. I say that Jenn's faith in Jesus carried her through most of her life, especially the hard parts, including the loss of her son Hudson and her cancer battle. But hers was not an idealized faith; it was a real faith. I say that Jenn knew she was a deeply loved daughter of God, yet she wrestled with God. She grieved before God. She was real and raw and sometimes angry with God—something only those who are deeply intimate and close with Jesus can be.

I also tell them that Jenn worked hard to intentionally choose hope in Christ day after day. She claimed the truth of Romans 8 over herself: that nothing, not even cancer, would separate her from the love of God in Christ Jesus. I say that she purposed, deliberately, *to do the next right thing* moment by moment.

I tell them that through it all Jenn loved and worshiped Jesus faithfully. She held on to his victory on the cross. She held on to the hope of heaven like an anchor for her soul. And I share this story: After finding out she was going on hospice, Jenn confided in me, "Aubs, it's not the miracle I wanted. It didn't end in redemption." And I said, gently, "I know, babe, but this is *the* actual redemption."

I tell all the funeral goers that Jenn has experienced Ultimate Redemption now. She is, at last, whole and healed and held by God. She is with Jesus, her Savior and Victor, the Lover of her soul. She is with her sweet baby boy, Hudson. And, if there is such a thing, she is hosting themed dance parties in heaven. I add, "It's not the miracle *we* wanted, but it is the truest redemption there is."

To honor the dead is a bewildering burden to bear. If anyone else had spoken at her funeral, I would have been so angry. But it is also the hardest thing I have ever done in my entire life, and I don't wish it on anyone. No one should have to honor their best friend at her funeral. We should honor our best friends at their eighty-fifth birthdays. We should toast to their wrinkles and arthritis and their bad backs.

The night after the funeral I dream of her again. This time, it is a peaceful dream. I am seated on the grass in some dreamlike park, or maybe a graveyard, actually. I am just sitting there, thinking about her, when she shows up and sits right by me. She is healthy and full and blonde, like before she had cancer, and I say, "Oh, hi. How are you feeling?"

She replies, "I am good. The cancer is gone."

I don't think it is a lucid dream, but in my dream, I realize something. "Wait. You died. Didn't you? So this is a dream, isn't it?" I ask.

She replies, "Yes, it is a dream."

Then I ask, "How is heaven? What is it like?"

And she says, "It's everything you could imagine."

Then I put my head on her shoulder and just rest there until I wake up.

Jenn has not departed; she has arrived. I believe that. But my friend should be here. We should be resting our heads on each other's shoulders for the next four decades.

☾

The day after the funeral is my lowest day. The gravity of it all pushes down on me heavily, pinning me to the couch for the entire day. I do not stop crying except to doze on and off, but I can't sleep, not really. I yell. I actually punch a wall, and I am not a wall-punching person. The boys see me like this when they leave for school and then again as they come home that afternoon. "Mom, are you still on the couch?"

"Yes, but I'll get up soon. I'll make dinner."

I don't. But thankfully, someone—I still don't know who—drops off dinner, and when Kevin comes home from work, he sits with me on the couch in the dark. And then, finally, finally, I say I need to sleep.

Mostly, now, I wonder what I am supposed to do with grief as it empties me out. Some say grief will become my life's companion. I personally find that grief is less companion and more disrupter, intruder, taking up space anytime she pleases. I am ambushed by grief when I am least ready for her. When I am getting ready for church or work. When I need to run to the pharmacy. When I have to sit in the waiting room at one of my son's orthodontist appointments. When I have other priorities. Grief is selfish and unaware, or at least deeply unconcerned with my schedule and my to-do list. Feral creature that she is, grief will not be tamed.

Grief changes us. One illustration depicts grief as a ball in a box with an alarm button attached to one side.[1] The box represents the soul. Initially, the ball of grief is so big that it continually hits the "alarm button." That alarm button activates our ambushy grief—uncontrollable tears, waves of overwhelming sadness, confusing brain fog, nausea, and more. And because the grief ball is so big, there is not much room for anything else in our soul-box. But as time passes, the illustration suggests, the grief ball will grow smaller. Then there is room in the soul for other things besides grief. There is more room for delights and enjoyments, for new experiences. Yes, grief will still hit the alarm button occasionally, but not nearly as often as it does in the early days.

I like that idea, that grief may one day bounce around in a lesser space of our souls. I sort of need that to hold on to, to be able to function right now in my fog of sadness. But I also wonder if it's quite right. Does the ball of grief really get smaller? Or does the box get bigger?

If what Paul says in Romans is true, that suffering produces character, perseverance, and hope (Romans 5:3-4), then maybe as we carry grief with us—each time the ball hits and sounds the alarm—the grief doesn't shrink, but the walls of the box enlarge. Maybe our capacity for resilience, our capacity to face the unspeakable, grows.

St. John of the Cross says that we come face-to-face with three theological virtues in the dark night: faith, hope, and charity.[2]

And each of these three virtues *requires* emptiness. If faith could be understood, then it would not be faith. If hope were something we could possess, then it would not be hope. Real charity, or love for God, cannot occur unless we withdraw our affection from false attachments, idols, distractions. For John, our growth in all three virtues—faith, hope, and love—can *only occur* when we find ourselves being emptied. Can *only* occur in dark nights.

So yes, in the upside-down way of Jesus, grief has a way of expanding and increasing our souls, our hearts, our compassion, and our depths—even as it empties us.

But also, maybe grief isn't a ball at all. And maybe there's no box. Maybe grief is a river, and your soul is the stone that grief smooths throughout the decades and changing seasons. Or maybe your soul is the river itself, and grief clears the debris, the unnecessary. Or maybe grief is a nighttime fireworks display, and your soul is a bunch of rockets exploding, and the embers falling, and sometimes the music, too. All you can do is take part in the explosiveness of it all. The people around you see the spectacle. All you know is that you are raining fire.

Whatever it is—box, river, explosion, or something else entirely—we will love others better because we appreciate empathy in a new way. We understand that everyone is carrying heavy and hard burdens. We enter into the hard stories of others with more kindness and patience. We show ourselves more grace. We connect more intimately with the sufferings of Jesus. We hope with more longing for the new creation of Jesus—that future promise of All Things New, All Wrongs Right. We develop a gravitas and a righteous anger, a new fire to see justice roll down, because we know things now, in grief, that we didn't know before. We know *pain* we didn't know before. And we appreciate life's mundane moments of splendor with new eyes. We know greater faith, hope, and love.

We know, that is, if we let grief do its work—if we keep showing up to God, ourselves, the outside world, and each other, even when we can't see God, understand ourselves, leave the safe confines of our bedrooms, or face others.

That seemingly mundane fact—that one's soul has the capacity to grow while facing excruciating pain and horrific loss—is a marvel. This is God's collision with death. God's opposition to death. God's authority over death. God's counterliturgy to the reductive tactics of death. This is the gospel's way of neutralizing death's ravenous *taking*: In Jesus, our hearts and our souls, our resilience and our compassion, will grow so big that we can never be consumed.

And, of course, all this soul growth matters, like, in the Grand Scheme of Things, which is probably why I am reminding us both of it, you and me.

But I also just want my friend back, as I am sure you also want your profound losses restored.

Wouldn't that be the better counteraction to death? That our people never leave us? Wouldn't that make much more sense? If cancer didn't exist? If death didn't occur? If we never had to give another eulogy? Face another child loss? Witness another injustice? If we never had to say goodbye to a dream, a longing, another lost thing?

If the soul's expansion entails our hearts being ripped out of our bodies, then I wonder if it's worth it. It seems to me there's a fine line between growth and breaking, and I don't know why one has to feel so much like the other.

☽

It's now a week after the funeral, or it might be two years since the funeral, or maybe three hours after. I don't know. Time is still a nothing. Whenever it is, I find myself unexpectedly texting Justin this afternoon. "This may sound weird, but I need to be surrounded by her things. Can I come write there? You won't even know I was there."

"Of course. That makes sense," he responds immediately. "That's a good idea."

Justin's grief is demonstrably more weighty, heavy, and intimate than mine. But I appreciate that he doesn't look sideways at my pain or roll his eyes at my emotions. He isn't comparing our grief. Without any questions, he understands why I need to write while being surrounded by Jenn's coffee mugs and art and cozy blankets.

So I am sitting at her dining room table, writing. This is a table she designed herself, a table she could never decide on the right finish for, so it remains unstained and covered with a tablecloth. On the wall in front of me is a piece of art that Jenn made, a beautiful wreath wrapped in burlap ribbon. Underneath it, she painted Acts 2:46: "They broke bread in their homes and ate together with glad and sincere hearts."

Jenn dreamt of having friends and family over on Sunday afternoons, of having an Acts 2 church in her own home. This wreath, this Scripture, and this frame are broken hallelujahs, and I am sitting here at her dining room table once again bowled over by the fact that she has gone. She is gone. Just so gone.

I spend a few quiet hours here, in the space where Jenn used to live, crying, remembering, working. And as I sit here, I realize I'm livid at death.

I am ready for a drunken pub brawl with death. I want to get my knuckles bloody, to smash some Guinness glasses over death's skull. I can see why the New Testament authors often refer to death as a force, as the last great enemy. Death is vile, evil. Death takes and takes without apology.

But there's something else, I am also realizing, something new. I am fearful about death, and that's different for me. Jenn's death has shaken me, shattered my equilibrium, stolen my courage. I am scared of what death means, of what dying is. I am afraid of the nothingness of it all when I think about it for too long. So I don't know who would win in the bar fight.

I have believed and proclaimed for most of my life that death has been defeated in Jesus' own death and resurrection. And I still do. I still want to. I still choose to. But, honestly, death feels like the victor right now.

At some point, I look out the back window and realize it's getting late and it's snowing—big, fluffy flakes. A soft, downy bedspread covers the barren branches outside, a new layer of winter for spring to battle its way through next year. It's not lost on me that later tonight the moon and stars will shine on this fresh blanket. It will sparkle.

I am imploding with grief, but in moments like this, something else is happening. I don't know if my soul is expanding, but it *is* searching: searching for meaning, for consequence in death.

That *something* within us keeps hunting for hope, for import, for beauty even when we think we have lost all capacity to do so—even when we are afraid of our quiet doubts, even when our fears are wrapped in mourning clothes. What does that search signify if not an increased capacity, a growing soul? That's got to mean God's presence is on the move here, right?

Admittedly, any answer I try to come up with rings tone-deaf against the cries of my grief. It ends up sounding offensive to my ears. It feels like a version of spiritual bypassing. I suppose it's enough to notice that my soul is grasping onto kite strings of promise without resolving the *why* of it all. It's not like there's any solving grief anyway.

I start to pack up to head home before the roads get bad, but I don't want to go. I want to crawl into Jenn's bed and smell her clothes and sip from her coffee cups. I won't do that, but I will do the dishes before I go because I can tell Justin is behind.

Then I'll close the door and leave a part of my heart here at her dining room table, looking out her back window, remembering our decades of chats on her back porch, remembering her kicking the soccer ball with her kids and mine, remembering our outdoor movie nights, remembering her laughter, her prayers, her vibrancy forever.

It is the still of the night.

My Jonathan has died.

I am full of sorrow.

It is snowing outside.

And somehow, impossibly, I notice.

PART THREE

NIGHT-LIGHTS

And he made the stars.
God placed them in the heavenly sky
to light up Earth
And oversee Day and Night.
GENESIS 1:16-18, MSG

LORD, you are the God who saves me;
day and night I cry out to you.
PSALM 88:1

A LITURGY FOR WHAT WE FIND IN THE DARK

Though the darkness hide thee, O God,
we trust that your presence is in the dark, as it is in the light.
But we have known your absence too long now
and we are desperate for some illumination.
We long to find you in some brighter place, especially after our long tunnels of night.

Command lights to twinkle again.
Elucidate meaning once more.
Relocate our lost things.
Or if not,
show us how to appreciate new things when we don't want to look forward.
Teach us to make discoveries in the dark.
Mostly, O God, bring respite to our souls, for we are weary from night travel.

O Jesus, Seeker and Finder and Lover of Things Lost in the Dark,
prompt our hearts to hope even as we lament.
Teach our bodies to inhale brilliance and brightness,
even as we exhale the ways seasons of death and darkness have marked us.
Please, O God, let it be true; that what we find in the dark is you.

12

FLOATING LANTERNS

When You're Not Ready to Say Goodbye (or Hello)

It's been seven years since we, my husband and I, along with an incredible team, planted a church—a beautiful, beloved community. Seven, Scripture implies, is a time of rest, of sabbaticals and clean slates and creation.

Those who study ancient numerology believe seven is the perfect number, one of fullness and, in some traditions, discovery. But in this, the seventh year of our church plant, the Year of Fullness and Discovery and Sabbath, or whatever you make of it, we find ourselves—like so many other churches in the postpandemic world—unexpectedly rebuilding, replanting, restarting. Those same "number" people say year eight is the year of new beginnings. I don't know, but I hope so.

Tonight, in fact, we are circled up with ministry team leaders, church friends, and other faithful folks to dream together about what God may have in store for years eight through fourteen. We are brainstorming and praying and Expo-markering on whiteboards, imagining wonderful new dreams together: future neighborhood outreaches, deep relationships, God's name glorified, conversion growth, the Spirit moving in our town, immigration reform, racial reconciliation, decolonization, equity, and love—Jesus' holistic love and salvation centering it all. *What will God do next?* is the feeling in the air. We are all expectant, excited like little kids at a birthday party.

Well, *they* are all expectant. I can't quite summon the excitement.

I get it. It's like our church family has been huddled under a makeshift rain shelter, hiding from a yearslong thunderstorm. The rain has finally slowed down, and we're tiptoeing out to splash in the puddles. We are peeling off and casting aside rain gear, shaking out umbrellas. In Chicago, it's still very cold outside, but in here, our church offices are filled with a fresh spring effervescence. We, all of us, are a church family, a team on mission. We are ready to do life in Christ together again after this horrific pandemic and season of collective grief has robbed us of so much. *Okay, next seven years—we're ready for you!*

If seven is a full-circle year, I suppose it makes sense. It also doesn't make any sense, however, because I am still out of body, watching it all happen. There's something in me that knows this is *good,* this moment is meaningful and special. But I can't bring myself to care. Because in the middle of all this, there's Jenn.

My best friend has always attended these kinds of meetings with me; she has never *not* been at my side at ministry events. She has never *not* processed and prayed and replayed and helped unpack church stuff with me. I don't want to open my heart to new people, or new dreams of the future, when my soul sister was just taken from me.

I am afraid to hope.

After loss, I am terrified to dream again with a new group of people, and even more terrified to let new friends in. So often in life we're told to *have thick skin*. But my skin is thin, okay? Thinner than it's ever been. And to open up, even the teensiest portal to what's underneath, means opening up to pain again, and maybe I've had enough hurt for a lifetime.

Whether you've lost someone to death or lost something that meant something to you, the choice to start over or to step forward or to be brave is a bit like voluntarily lying down on a surgical table without knowing if you are under the care of a skilled surgeon or a hack. Hopefully the heart transplant goes okay, but you don't really know if it will. It's all a life-threatening risk.

Can we dream again without getting crushed? Can we love again without pain? Can we put our hearts on the line without having them break?

When my cousin Cameron died tragically while snowshoe hiking in Crater Lake, we lit floating lanterns at his funeral. It was a small way to ritualize our saying goodbye. It was lovely, watching them light up the darkness. But it was dreadful, too, because it signified a letting go. A releasing. An ending of life and relationship and future. We sent the floating lanterns off while sobbing, drunk on our sorrows. No one should have to do that. We shouldn't have to say a ceremonial or final goodbye to those we love.

Basically, I am scared.

Scared to say goodbye.
Scared to say hello.

Scared to hope.
Scared overall.

Somewhere, far away, in a forlorn, forgotten hallway of my heart, filled with all the ghosts of loss, I can sense Jesus saying something in all this, something *about* all this. But I am still in the dark night, still not quite able to hear, or maybe too angry to answer. Jesus took my best friend from me and then seemingly stopped speaking to me during one the saddest, hardest seasons of my life—ghosted me during this dark night of the soul. I am not entirely sure I am ready to listen to that voice.

Still, I think about when Jesus appeared to his disciples after his resurrection. They mistook him for a ghost. Luke, who wrote this story down, describes the disciples as being "startled and frightened" at the sight of Jesus. But Jesus assured them, "Why are you troubled . . . ? Look at my hands and my feet. . . . Touch me and see; a ghost does not have flesh and bones, as you see I have" (Luke 24:37-39).

There will always be ghosts that haunt us and fears that follow us. There will always be reasons to shut down your heart and turn off your dreamer, never imagining or experiencing something new and alive again. But ghosts and fears are not Jesus.

This is where we reach an intolerable impasse, a catch-22, grief's tautology: Choosing to love again or dream again or play again or try again will always require the courage to grieve again.[1] Entering into new friendships, rejoining life, being in and with community, reaching out of our pain into the pain of others: These are the things that begin to mend our heartache but also the very things that threaten to rupture us again. Loving will inevitably lead to more losing, but to choose not to love or enter in is certainly another kind of death.

Which is worse? The threat of grief happening again or the threat of your soul shriveling in isolation, loneliness, detachment? That voice in the hall, along with life itself, seems to be asking an impudent question: *Can you do it scared? Can you choose hope again, even while afraid? Can you gradually and gently try once more?*

•

In your dark night, some lights might begin to dapple your path now and then. One of those lights is this invitation to reenter community after your loss. It may be a long time before you feel ready for this, ready to say hello to new people, new memories, new dreams. Because you are someone who has borne loss, ultimately other people will look to you for clues about how to process suffering, and that can be a good thing. When you are ready, you will find friends who can hold your pain as you bear witness to theirs. You will minister healing, hope, and faith to one another. A beautiful, beloved community can form from loss. It can. And that is a strange gift of grief. One day, you may feel ready for that. But there is no rush. I know it's hard to believe right now, but your courage will return in due time, however timidly.

In late March, just a few short weeks after this church meeting, I fly to Dallas for a girls' weekend, to meet up with some friends from grad school. As I step off the plane onto the bridgeway, I feel Jenn with me, as she has been with me on so many other girls' trips throughout our friendship. Real or imagined, I feel her with me. So I have a conversation with her as I walk off the plane. To my own shock, I whisper aloud, "You aren't allowed to come with me on this trip. I will pick you up again on my way home. But I must do this without you."

I did not expect that. I didn't expect to send the ghost of my best friend away so boldly. I felt like I was betraying her. But there was this base instinct that rose up in me and declared, decisively, *She cannot go on this trip with you, Aubrey. She can never go on another trip with you, Aubrey. Because she is not here. You have to make new memories. You have to invest in other friendships. You are alive, and you have to keep living.*

A year from now, I go on another road trip with a close friend. While cruising down the road, we sing at the top of our lungs to '90s female power ballads. We eat gas station snacks and take selfies and create new inside jokes. We make a tentative plan to do it again the following year.

When I return home from that trip, I dream that Jenn breaks into my house and steals some of my household decorations. When I confront her in the dream, she tells me it's because they are tacky. But I know the truth: She is mad at me for moving on. Or maybe I feel guilty for moving on. Or, more likely, I am still terrified of it. I'd rather stay frozen in time. I want to become like Han Solo, captured in carbonite.

All the while, stars blink awake at night and close their eyes each morning, and do it all again and again. Time strides ever onward, inviting us to keep pace. Life beckons us forward. Even the dark night eventually moves sunward. But it's all happening much too fast.

Grief makes you want to grasp time like an hourglass in your hand. But time is sand through your fingers; it is never the glass itself.

13

NORTHERN LIGHTS

Unexpected Finds in the Dark

One morning, a new friend sends me a voice message. I really like her. But I am so often perched on a brittle branch of worry: *Will she like me the way Jenn did? Will anyone? Will I be lonely forever?* Fear makes it hard to enter in relationally and to relate with vulnerability.

"How are you?" she asks, checking in on my grief. She is out on a walk as she messages me, and I can hear the birdsong and the breeze in the background, her breathing deliberate and shaky from her swift stride in the brisk spring air.

"I am doing great!" I start to respond in my voice message back. "Things are a little hard, but mostly I see God doing good thi—"

I interrupt myself. I am overcompensating, pretending to be okay when I am absolutely not okay.

So I pause. Inhale deeply. Exhale slowly. Clear my throat. Begin again.

"Here's a truer answer. I am tired emotionally and pretty tender today. Thank you for checking in."

Something in the birdsong and breeze in the background of her message makes me think about Adam and Eve and God "strolling in the garden in the evening breeze" (Genesis 3:8, MSG). I wonder what the *sound of God strolling* is like. Maybe God sounds just like us, a sauntering rustle through grass and leaves. Or maybe the sound of God strolling is something else entirely, like the sound of sea turtles swimming through an ocean current, the sound of stars colliding in another galaxy.

I don't know what the sound of God strolling is like, but for some reason, this thought does something in me, awakens a long-dormant instinct: I want to find God in the darkness. I am sick and tired of not finding God in the darkness.

Where are you, God?

I've been asking but unable to see. Unable to hear. Unable to discover any crumbs of hope in such a long time.

Something in me decides *today* to start paying better attention, to get curious again.

I suddenly feel like a novice detective. I am Harriet the Spy opening her composition book and pulling the pencil out from behind her ear. I have decided to put a glass against the door of life and strain my ear to hear something good.

I start by going back through memories, journals, all the writing I did in the middle of the night when grief wouldn't let me sleep. I mine it all, looking for the ways God showed up when I wasn't willing or able to notice. I also begin intentionally opening my eyes for new discoveries in the dark.

When you're sadder, lonelier, and more confused than you have ever been, when loss has stolen your person, your dreams, your will, and your faith, when you are on a precipice—go on a hunt for found things. Things Found in the Dark is more than a clunky list. For the heartbroken night wanderer, a list of found things is a way to tune the soul to the sound of God. A list of found things is a tiny way for the disengaged to gently reengage with life. A list of found things is faith when you have none.

Here are the first four items on mine:

1. *The letter.* One afternoon, a few weeks after Jenn's passing, we arrive home after spending time with Justin and the boys, and there is an envelope lying out on the middle of my kitchen island. An envelope with Jenn's familiar, loopy handwriting on it.

   It is an old card, sent a couple of years ago. It begins with "My precious friend." In it, Jenn is thanking me for loving her family and taking care of her when she was first diagnosed with cancer. It is full of soft, kind words.

   This card wasn't there before we went to see Jenn's boys. But it is here now.

   Before Jenn died, we joked about her haunting people. She said, "I would never do that; I would never scare anyone." So I don't think this is a haunting. Maybe the wind blew the letter from its resting place in my kitchen catchall, or maybe someone put it there and forgot. All I know is that a letter from my best friend, thanking me for loving her family, was *just conspicuously out* on my countertop when I returned from doing just that—spending the day loving her family.

I might sound superstitious or crazy. But maybe the veil between here and her is thin. Maybe God's love reaches across that invisible boundary line, reminding us that we are seen and not alone in our pain.

I jot this down on my list: God surprises us in the dark night, letting us know we are seen.

2. *Directives from friends.* I spend the week before Jenn's funeral fretting that I don't have the right bra or outfit or shoes to wear. In fact, I have several dreams about showing up to her service in entirely inappropriate attire. So I try to go shopping.

   Do not go shopping in early grief. You will make decisions like a zombie, but a zombie with big emotions, a zombie in a grief fog. You will make bad decisions, all while watching yourself make those bad decisions, unable to stop them from happening.

   I end up buying seven pairs of black boots to try on with the dress I am planning to wear for the funeral. Not one. Not two. *Seven.*

   I know I am not searching for items; I am searching for Jenn. I am looking for hope.

   I finally text my friend Hollie for help:

   I can't make a decision.

   Which boots should I get?

   I can't keep all seven.

   I think I have grief brain.

She responds,

> Get the leather boots with the zipper and move on. Those are cute. Get some tights and try them on with your black dress and your camo sweater. We'll all be wearing camo to honor Warrior Wednesday. That's a good outfit for the funeral.

Then,

> Be kind to yourself.

Clarity from friends. Is this the sound of God's love in the dark night too? I write this down so I will remember it: In grief, God provides us with wise people of clarity, friends who help us take a next small step.

3. *The hawk.* It's Galentine's Day. Jenn's holiday.[1] This was her day to celebrate the women in her life, especially the single moms. Today sucker punches me. But I have to pull myself together to go to work.

   As I back out of my driveway, I notice a hawk perched on my front porch railing, just staring at my front door. Later, a friend stops by my house and sends me a photo. *Did you know there is a hawk staring at your house?* This afternoon, the hawk has moved to the tree in my front yard, still watching my house. The next day, it is gone. I haven't seen it since.

   That same friend sends me a text: *Do you know that*

the hawk is often considered a sign from heaven, a sign of protection?

And look—I know, I know. There was probably an unsuspecting mouse or squirrel that my hawk was hunting. And there are all those theological debates about "signs from beyond."

But also, maybe God does this kind of inexplicable thing, especially when we hurt so deeply. So I add this to my list of found things: God gives us signs and wonders. Some might think these are just coincidences. But I don't. Not today.

4. *Sabbath delight.* Today, on a girls' trip to a mountain resort just outside Seattle, I am Sabbathing with my dear friends Hollie and Kathy, those closest to Jenn besides me. I didn't realize we were Sabbathing at the time, but I do as I look back on the day we spent together:

   I wrote outside in the morning while drinking coffee.

   We went on a hike, soaking in the creation beauty of the mountains.

   We went to lunch and visited a local bookstore.

   We sat at a coffee shop, enjoying iced lattes and chatting.

   We drove around looking at the Pacific Northwest's luscious scenery—the rivers, the mountains, the farmlands.

   We stopped at a farm stand for local fruit—peaches and Washington cherries.

   We actually threw axes. (I hit *several* bull's-eyes. Like, I might be a *natural* axe thrower.)

   We laughed and played and ate a backyard dinner of charcuterie.

We ended our Sabbath with an evening ride on electric scooters and a hot-tub sit.

It was a full day but not a busy day. The hours were luxurious. And I haven't rested, I realize, in so long. Since Jenn died, my internal motor has been on, always on, driving me even while in idle. This has been my body's defense against time, against grief.

I add this to my list as well: stillness, surrender, pleasure, playfulness—these can be found in our dark nights when we are ready for them.

☾

My list of lost things is longer than my list of found things, or at least it's heavier, weighted on that side. But I have these found things, and they have given me a taste for more. I am Jacob, and *I will not let life go unless it blesses me.*

For life does bless if we look for it.

The purple irises and powder blue hydrangeas in our garden refuse to stop flourishing. Thunderstorms arrive, terrifying us, then lose ground to a peaceful morning sky. My body grows tired at night, then miraculously automatically wakes up each new day. The chipmunk who lives on our porch (we've named him Theodore) keeps chirping us awake every morning. New movies get released. New albums come out. The sun still rises, that show-off. With her daily rituals, ordinary demands, and quotidian gestures, life extends an altar call to those of us lost in our dark nights. *Rise up. Come forward. Be found.*

And God knows we are limited. We are flesh and sinews and sadness and frailty. We need guideposts in our grief. We need northern lights in our dark night. We need dynamic patterns of luminescence to move us from our disbelief, doubt, and disillusionment toward *wonder*. A step closer. A breath closer. A thin line closer.

As people of faith, we are so often called on pilgrimage; called to go when we can't see the way forward; called to step out without knowing the conditions; called to dive deeper even when it's scary. Grief is its own kind of pilgrimage. Your job, when you are ready, is to start looking. Notice the ways God is coming toward you in the darkness with love.

Which reminds me: There's something else I might add to my list.

On her hospice bed, Jenn and I exchanged *I love you*s again and again. We shared sacred secrets. And Jenn—maybe delusional from morphine, maybe totally sober-minded, but either way most definitely out of some source prophetic and holy, from the deep well of love within her—said, "It is okay to be sad. But you best celebrate, girl. Don't forget to celebrate."

To deliberately look for goodness, to try your best to search for delight, to fight to celebrate once you've been marked ineradicably by death and loss is no easy undertaking. Right now, my yes is a whimper, not a shout, not a declaration. I am limping my way to life's altar, my Goliath grief in one hand, my pocket-sized list of found things in the other.

And all the while, God is strolling with me, as God is strolling with you, as we hold space for hard things, as we take brave new steps forward—one birdsong, one breeze, one beauty hunt, one tiny break in the armor at a time.

14

ILLUMINATIONS

Stripping Away Pretense, Reclaiming Your Voice and Agency

I have a memory, a dark one. For the past several years, this memory has budged at the door of my subconscious, trying to edge its way through. But I have never been ready, so I always slam the door shut, bolting it for good measure. Ever since Jenn died, though, the dark memory has been returning, practically banging down the door. *Pay attention to me. Pay attention to me. Pay attention to me.*

In a memory before the dark memory, I am maybe eight or nine years old, triangle elbows and skinned knees, rope for hair. I love Care Bears and My Little Ponies and riding bikes with my next-door neighbor Brady. I also have another neighborhood friend—we will call her Ainsley—who is several years older than me, a teenager. She is so cool, it makes no sense why she comes over every day after school to play with me.

One afternoon, the three of us—Brady, Ainsley, and I—spend hours riding our bikes through a homemade obstacle course. The course itself is unfussy, almost boring, just some mini orange cones and Hula-Hoops sporadically strewn around the driveway. But other neighborhood kids have gathered to ride bikes through our project, and we are awarded pride of place in the cul-de-sac. Overall, it is turning into one of those iconic neighborhood days.

The three of us are leaning against our bikes, surveying our course, when—in the middle of this epic neighborhood day, in front of all the other cul-de-sac kids—Ainsley asks if I like Brady. *Out loud.* An announcement.

"Do you like Brady?"

Then Ainsley leans in and whispers conspiratorially so Brady and the other kids can't hear: "Say yes if you don't like him. Say no if you do."

I don't think I have to tell you—this is a Sophie's choice. Say yes aloud: everybody, the entire neighborhood, thinks I like Brady. Say no: Ainsley thinks I do. And I don't want her to think I do because, well, I don't.

Do I save face in front of the cul-de-sac kids or my cool teenager friend? Those are the stakes.

So I choose the truth. Sort of. I say no and I mean no. But Ainsley turns my no into a yes.

"I knew you liked him!" she blurts out loud enough for all the other kids to hear. "See, Brady, I told you!"

This is when my confusion about yeses and nos is born. I know, of course, that sometimes people fib or stretch the truth, but today, this very day, is when I learn you can say one thing and mean another, or mean one thing but say another, and that sometimes you do it just to survive.

Almost four decades after that no-means-yes day, I am bringing the other, darker memory to my spiritual director, Ben. A noise machine is whirring in the background of his office to block any distracting sounds, and I am seated on his couch, my two feet planted firmly on the carpet in front of me. My hands are clenched fists in my lap.

You see, I can no longer ignore the dark memory. I am beginning to realize that the dark night of the soul does this. It's like grief silences some of the extraneous nonsense in your life, and the lost items that have been hidden in back closets or stuck on dusty shelves can begin shuffling forward, rattling—demanding to be opened and examined.

It is a challenge to talk about this memory with Ben. It's a challenge to type the words now. At some point that summer, Ainsley moved from friend to mean girl to predator. She convinced me that I wanted to do things I didn't want to. She let my no mean yes, and I went along with it.

I blurt all this out to Ben, who assures me that I don't need to feel ashamed or anything. "But I don't," I explain, unclenching my fists and tucking my hair behind my ears. "It's not that. That's not why the memory is bugging me. I don't feel scarred or anything. I know it wasn't my fault. I also know she was probably a victim herself. But something about it is poking at me, and I can't find the needle."

He is taking notes on a yellow legal pad and asks some guiding questions, a bit like a therapist: "Have you felt that way again? Have you experienced anything similar before?" When I can't answer, he says, tenderly, "Let's be quiet for a moment and see what the Spirit reveals."

I readjust my position on Ben's couch, cross and uncross my

ankles, then plant my feet firmly on the ground again. Breathing in and out, asking the Spirit to help me find the lost thing that's in this memory. *God, where are you? God, what are you showing me?* Slowly and gradually, memories float through my awareness like flotsam: the time I let someone stay at my home for a summer when I didn't want them to. The guys I dated before Kevin that I didn't like. The commitments to events or meetings or people I didn't have time or capacity for.

How is *any* of this related to Ainsley?

I start to open my mouth to ask Ben what he thinks, but the realization hits before I even speak the words. "Oh my gosh. It's not shame. It's not that. It's . . . oh my gosh." My voice quivers, and I have to pause for a moment quietly before I can finish my sentence.

Finally, I cross my arms over my chest and sit up a little straighter. When I speak again, my voice is filled with certainty, a verdict: "It's that I haven't said no when I've wanted to. I didn't kick Ainsley out of my house. I didn't tell anyone. And I have *not* said no to so many things. I have not claimed my opinion or used my own voice . . . and I am angry about it."

As I say these words aloud, I realize the dark night has illuminated something at last. I have been that proverbial frog in a pot of increasingly hot water. But my capacity for taking on hotter and hotter temperatures while being polite about it has finally reached its boiling point. Unlike the frog, what's boiling is my rage—and it's feeling pretty good to finally get heated.

In response to my anger, Ben says something supremely obvious, but it nonetheless devastates me in the best possible way: "Here is what I have learned over the years. If it's not an unadulterated yes, it's an absolute no." Then he helps me write down a few sentences, truths that I regularly speak over myself: "I have agency. I am deeply loved by God. And I can say yes or no to anything so that I can take up space and remain faithful to God's call on my life."

As I drive home after that session, I am amped up. I remember something Jenn said before she passed: "You're a really good cheerleader for others, but I also want you to learn to stop people pleasing."

I was a little offended, admittedly. Then I reconsidered because she was right: I have been afraid to assert myself, to disagree. I have spent most of my life saying yes when I wanted to say no, not expressing feelings when I have been upset, not standing up for myself when others are crossing boundaries. I've been passive with my concerns, agreeing to plans when I've needed rest, and, really, just cheering everyone on but myself.

It's so simple to recognize this, but the shift is tectonic. I am finding my agency, my best yeses and my nos. I am a mermaid, and I am finally taking my voice back from the sea witch who stole it.

So many of us feel like this—a little unsure of our voice, our place, our opinions. We doubt ourselves. We second-guess our value. We feel like imposters. We say yes when we want to say no. We were socialized not to let anyone down, or not to trust ourselves, or to say yes so people will like us, approve of us.

But then grief comes along and does two seemingly opposing things. Grief threatens to steal our resolve because the whole world is suddenly precarious, fragile, and uncertain. And somehow grief also disrupts our self-doubt and diffidence. We stop caring so much what other people think. We learn that what matters and what used to matter are sometimes entirely different things. And that new perspective grants us gumption, clarity, assurance, the ability to say what we mean and mean what we say.

❯

At least that's what I'm trying to do. Tonight I am speaking at a women's event on the North Shore of Chicago. North Shore women are bosses, fabulous in the best way, and they are in full array tonight—heels and power blazers, conversations about their new movies and other creative projects buzzing in the air. After the event, I'm standing around my book table, chatting with and praying for some of the attendees, when an older woman comes up behind me and gently taps me on the shoulder. I spin around to greet her, wide smile on my face. An observant onlooker might have noticed my smile turn stiff, because the first thing she says to me is "Well, aren't you cute." But she says it like she means the actual opposite of *cute*. She says "cute" in the most condescending tone imaginable.

From there, she gets meaner. She calls my message drivel and says, "How dare you stand there selling your books like you have something important to say?" And then, almost nonchalantly, she tells me her husband died last year. My compassion flag starts waving, because I know what fresh grief is like and I know that she is not really angry at me at all but at life, at God, at her own darkness. I say how sorry I am for her loss. She responds venomously: "You *should* be sorry."

That's when I remember: *Oh, wait. I have agency. I don't have to listen to this or take this.* So I open my mouth, and my mermaid voice actually works. "Ma'am, I am so sorry for your loss. But you're being rude, and you do not have permission to speak to me like this."

Then I turn my back to her, and she walks away harrumphing.

Can I just say? This moment is a triumph, a gorgeous execution. And it starts a domino effect. Days later, I am writing in a coffee shop when someone (who does not attend my church) sits down to complain about a program at my church. I forget for a second that I have agency, but then I remember. "You know what? These are not my work hours. This is my personal writing time. Why don't you schedule an appointment, and we can chat about your concerns in my office." Another triumph.

A few days after that, someone asks if I can help them host an event, and I can't because, well, I don't want to. So I say no. No, like a complete sentence.

A few months later, in late summer, I take my son Nolan to the local pool. He keeps begging me to do a cannonball. "Mom, come on, pleeeeeeease do a cannonball with me!"

The truth is, I am too insecure and self-conscious to do a cannonball as a middle-aged woman in a bathing suit. I am so aware of my aging body, and because of my autoimmune disease, my joints are often swollen and sore. Plus I must still have some of my nine-year-old self in me because, like her, I don't want to embarrass myself in front of the whole neighborhood.

So, initially, I leave my son to the cannonballs, choosing instead to sit on a lounge chair and read in the hot sun. But instead of reading, I just sit there adjusting and readjusting my body, sucking in my stomach, repositioning my legs, hoping to find a comfortable position to simply exist in the world as an adult woman. I am suddenly aware of how I have done this my entire life. I have tried to manage my body, my emotions, my opinions, my grief so that I am acceptable, polite, and sensible for others. But today, I recall my phrases: *I have agency. I am deeply loved by God. And I can say yes or no to anything so that I can take up space and remain faithful to God's call on my life.* And I want to say yes to my son. I do not exist as an apology. I don't need anyone's permission to live and thrive and splash in the water. I put my book down and yell to my son, "Okay, I will do a cannonball with you!"

I stand up to walk to the edge of the water, where my son is staring in disbelief. "Really, Mom? You're really going to do it?!"

This is not momentous for anyone watching, or rather, for anyone *not* watching—they are too busy being aware of their own bodies and insecurities and grief and worries. But this feels like the most audacious moment of my entire existence.

There's a scene in the classic '80s movie *Say Anything* where John Cusack, playing the iconic Lloyd Dobler, says to his sister (played by his real-life sister, Joan Cusack), "You used to be fun. You used to be warped and twisted and hilarious—and I mean that in the best way. I mean it as a compliment."

Her response? "I was hilarious once, wasn't I?"[1]

Maybe the dark night is Lloyd Dobler, beckoning us back to ourselves. Certainly a changed version, with tender places that weren't there before—but perhaps it's time to accept the invitation.

My grief has been a long run-on sentence, a Jack Kerouac novel, an Allen Ginsberg poem, moving forward and onward, line by unstructured line, descending the page with a general unruliness, maybe a few punctuation marks but no clear ending, no editorial organization, no big picture. This decision to do a cannonball is an exclamation point, a lightning strike, a protest sign. A valiant yes to life. A loud no to insecurity.

And so, with my wobbly body, shaky soul, and unedited grief in tow, I take a few steps back from the edge, get a running start, jump, and tuck in my knees, an inelegant missile rocketing into our neighborhood pool while my son cheers me on.

When I come up out of the water, sweeping my wet hair out of my eyes, a big, mischievous grin on my face, I notice that Nolan is laughing with delight. "Mom, I didn't think you'd really do it. I never actually thought you would."

"And why not?" I ask him, feeling a little sassy and proud of myself.

"I don't know. Just like your joints and life and stuff. I wasn't even sure if you could."

Yes, I think, *joints and life and stuff. I didn't know if I could either.*

Losing Jenn, holding my grief, trudging through the dark night—I feel like I have been walking around without skin. But this found thing—my voice, my agency, my yes when I mean yes—it's a new layer of epidermis. It is protection, permission.

I am Dorothy dazzling in color, finding her way home. I am Ariel reclaiming her voice and choosing a new life. I am Janis Joplin with a power chord, Taylor Swift with a turn of phrase, Ella Fitzgerald with a syncopated scat, Joey Ramone with the perfect punk-rock leather jacket—all of them stealing the show. I am Lloyd Dobler with a boom box, absolutely crushing the grand gesture.

What I mean is, my younger self can at last be brave and brash. Every time I say no *when I mean no* and yes *when I mean yes,* I retroactively hand my younger self a microphone and say, "Girl, the stage is yours. Make some noise." And, friends, that is some redemption in the darkness right there.

Loss may try to keep you small, silence you. But you have agency.

Grow raucous if you want to.

Or stay a whisper if that's more authentically you.

Either way, you are loved. You are invited to take up space. And you get to do whatever you want with both your yeses and your nos.

15

SATELLITES AND STARLIGHT

Waiting Patiently for the Lord

It is fall once more, and a friend invites us to the Dominican Republic, a place he lives nearly half the year and has fallen in love with. He has also fallen in love with a Dominican chef there named Nicole, the brightest sunshine of a woman. Nicole lost her best friend several years ago; her BFF's signature is tattooed on the inside of her wrist, braided with her forever. She and I understand each other, the way deep calls to deep, without having to say much about it.

Our friend, Chris, has been traveling to the Dominican Republic for the past twenty years in partnership with several orphanages and safe-haven schools, and he's been inviting us to his favorite island for about half those years. At long last, we are meeting him at O'Hare International Airport at the ungodly hour of 3:00 a.m. to board a 5:00 a.m. flight to Santiago. From Santiago, we make our way across the island to Jarabacoa, Constanza, and Monte Plata and then end our week in the capital, Santo Domingo. We see the oldest churches in Latin America. We eat plantains, yuca arepitas, massive avocados, carrots the size of shoeboxes, and, of course, rice and beans. We drink Dominican coffee and sip chinola juice. We witness injustice and pray for justice while grappling with what to do about it. We see precious, hurting children. We honor the faithful people who care for them, who advocate for them. At night, from the rooftop of our guesthouse, we stare at stars and satellites, sometimes mistaking one for the other. Starlight or satellite, the Dominican sky sparkles.

I can't say my own dark night is getting any brighter, can't tell you my grief is getting lighter. But as I look at the stars, I am increasingly on the lookout for new glimmers of hope. I am hollowed out but watching for wonder. And that's not nothing.

Nicole teaches us a Dominican expression: "Everybody's brave until the cockroach flies." We laugh at this turn of phrase until the night we scream when a bat flies through our house and we realize that the bat is a Dominican "cockroach." I get it. Certain things don't seem scary until you are forced to face their reality.

Something I have been afraid to face is that I feel betrayed by God. Betrayed that God let Jenn die. Betrayed that God hasn't drawn near to comfort me, except when I *really* look, and even then, it's just a few items on a list of found things that I am desperate to make. I want God to be more obvious, more present, more comforting, more available—but God hasn't been those things. At least, he hasn't felt that way.

Because of this, I haven't been able to open the Scriptures in about a year, at least not for personal communion with God. I am still a teaching pastor, so I read for study or preparation, but I used to connect with God through Bible reading. That time was refreshing for my soul, was one of my habits of faith, and it kept me close with God, worshiping God. But this year, opening Scripture has felt too intimate, too exposing. Like I can't let myself get that close to the one who has let me down. I walk by my well-loved Bible most mornings, where it has sat on the coffee table unmoved for nearly a year, and say aloud, "You just stay over there. I am not ready for you yet."

One night in the DR, I can't sleep, so I lie in bed watching a sci-fi movie on my iPad. I don't really get the plot, but it involves a woman hurtling violently through space in a mech suit, mostly screaming and breaking her bones as she thrashes around in the dark. I watch it with the volume down and subtitles on so I don't wake Kevin as he sleeps next to me. The descriptive captions all say something like *agonizing sobs* or *frightened groans* or *terrified screams. Oh girl,* I think as I watch, *same.* At some point, Kevin rolls over, eyes half-open, and asks what I'm watching. "A grief movie," I reply. Then I close the iPad cover and go to sleep, fitfully.

I've walked with Jesus a long time, through more than one painful season, so I am not necessarily a flight risk. I'm not running away from God or the Christian faith or the church or anything, but I am scared to open my Bible, afraid that if I try, God won't show up, the Spirit won't reveal anything, and I will feel more abandoned than I already do. But I'm also undeniably afraid of hurtling through this dark night with no end in sight. So the next morning, I wake up and tiptoe toward a risk. I open my Bible app and read Psalm 40, just the first three verses. But then I keep reading them, again and again and again. From Santiago to Santo Domingo, I just keep rereading this prayer, this song, borne from King David's own dark night of the soul.

I waited patiently for the LORD;
    he turned to me and heard my cry.
He lifted me out of the slimy pit,
    out of the mud and mire;
he set my feet on a rock
    and gave me a firm place to stand.
He put a new song in my mouth,
    a hymn of praise to our God.
Many will see and fear the LORD
    and put their trust in him.

As I read, I imagine David stuck at the bottom of a dark, damp cavern. He's hunched over, naked, hoping for some kind of rope ladder to appear so he can finally climb out. But something else grabs my attention, sparks my curiosity: the great inactivity of David at the bottom of his dark cistern, especially when compared to the action of God. It's not, I realize, all that different from when God wrestled with Jacob.

- God turns to David (Psalm 40:1).
- God hears his cry (Psalm 40:1).
- God lifts him out of the slimy pit (Psalm 40:2).
- God places his feet on solid ground (Psalm 40:2).
- God gives David a firm place to stand (Psalm 40:2).
- God puts a new song in his mouth (Psalm 40:3).
- God gives David a hymn of praise (Psalm 40:3).

In our dark nights, it's easy to become slightly obsessed with what we are doing or not doing. Are we dwelling too much in our pain? Are we moving too slow? Are we sadder than we should be? Are we annoying people or disappointing God with our grief? Are we *too much right now*? Are we not enough? Can we get through this? Are we failing? Are we fighting for hope enough?

But maybe into all our dark nights there arrives a day, an hour, a moment to finally release ourselves from unnecessary anxiety around all we are or aren't doing. There comes a time to focus, instead, on what God does in the dark.

In David's dark night, God stretches, inclines, bends low, draws near to help. God hears David's cries. God listens with intentionality. God raises David up, helps him ascend out of that pit, and establishes him once again on stable ground, places him in a secure stronghold. There's more: God gives the psalmist a new song of praise to add to his worship set. The *only* thing David does from the depths of his miry pit is this: wait patiently. Every other verb belongs to God.

The wording David uses of himself, translated as "wait patiently," is *qava* in Hebrew, which refers to waiting with hope. The related noun *tikvah* has the basic meaning "cord."[1] David the lyricist seems to be engaging in wordplay here. In his waiting patiently, there was still something God was doing, offering. David seems to be saying, *In my dark night, there was a cord keeping me connected to God. All I did was hold on until God tugged on that cord and pulled me out.*

•

As you wait patiently in your own dark night for whatever it is you are awaiting—the sense of God's presence to return, your heart to not hurt so acutely, the losses to be fewer than the finds—like me, you'll probably want to avoid intimacy with God. You'll be afraid. You'll lose your sense of wonder and curiosity. One minute you'll feel like you're plunging haphazardly through space and the next like you're cemented to the bottom of a pit. The waiting is slow work. So how do we do it?

What stars and satellites teach us is the profound relationship between contradictions. A satellite's orbit is made up of forward motion and dragging gravity. And stars . . . well, we see their brightest emissions as they age—indeed, as they die. Waiting patiently for God to show up in your dark night means learning to navigate push and pull, pausing and plodding, sunlight and starlight. And maybe if it feels like God has been withdrawing, it's because God is drawing you near.

Part of the dark night's purpose is to teach us that faith is not a feeling; it is a gift, a grace, a practice, *a way*. That means every act of ordinary faithfulness we participate in when we are in spiritual darkness—continuing to show up for our families and church communities, caring for neighbors, feeding the hungry, fighting for justice and equity, loving our spouses faithfully, living within our means, wrestling for hope, reading the Psalms as prayers—is a night-light in our dark. This might mean picking up some of the passive spiritual practices—those habits you *don't* do, things like silence, breath prayers, slowness, rest.[2] Or this might mean sinking to the bottom of your pit for a while, trusting that the hand on the other end of the cord will one day lift you out.

As for me, after Psalm 40, I turn back to Psalm 1. In time, I slowly read more psalms, and somehow, eventually, this prayer book for the people of God, this book that covers the gamut of human emotions, becomes my soul's sustenance, my daily breadcrumbs.

The psalms that stand out are the dark-night ones:

> Do not let the floodwaters engulf me
>   or the depths swallow me up
>   or the pit close its mouth over me.
>
> PSALM 69:15

> When I was in distress, I sought the Lord;
>   at night I stretched out untiring hands,
>   and I would not be comforted.
>
> PSALM 77:2

> He made the moon to mark the seasons,
>   and the sun knows when to go down.
> You bring darkness, it becomes night.
>
> PSALM 104:19-20

I return again and again to the dark-night cries of Psalm 40:17:

> But as for me, I am poor and needy;
>   may the Lord think of me.
> You are my help and my deliverer;
>   you are my God, do not delay.

Yes, God. No more delay.

I finish all 150 psalms, then I read through the book again. Then again. At first I'm just marking each one with the date I read it. Soon I start to add a thought. *I still miss Jenn.* Or *God, when will you answer me?* Or *Is this a promise or just a turn of phrase?*

Then eventually an *Amen.* Once I even wrote, *Whoa. Thank you, God.*

Not doing it perfectly. Not rigidly. Not even profoundly.

Patiently. Waiting*ly*. Openly.

This minuscule habit seems just that, infinitesimal. But through it, I find that my soul is an inchworm. Segment by segment, space by space, I inch again toward the presence of God.

Or maybe, bit by bit, God is reminding me that he never actually went away.

☾

Since losing Jenn, I have been wearing two bracelets made of thin cords. One says *strength*, each letter a bead. The other *ride or die* in honor of our friendship. When I return home from my trip to the DR and begin unpacking my luggage, the *ride or die* bracelet snaps, its beads spilling all over my closet floor.

I don't know if you're a dramatic person, if you take things like that in stride or if they make you fall to your knees with tears. But I slump to my knees, picking up the beads one by one. I sit there on my closet floor, sobbing, holding these remains of my best friendship with no idea what to do with them. I finally grab a little painted jewelry box, one I purchased a few years ago at a boutique off Route 66. It is white and silver, decorated with little bluebirds, and I actually bought twin jewelry boxes that day—one for me and the other for Jenn. I place the bracelet's cord and its detached beads in my tiny bird box, hoping it will serve as a sort of connector, keeping me bonded to my friend, to memories, to love. It's not lost on me, the symbolism—my ride-or-die is gone. But the strength cord remains.

Some things don't seem scary until you are forced to face them. You and I, we've been traveling together for a while now through twilight and dusk, through darkest night, through loss and grief and doubt and all that goes with it—and I hope your night is lightening even a bit. I hope the bottom of your pit is not as muddy as it could be. But if you are still scared to face some hard realities, that's okay too. Again, you get to be right where you are for as long as you need to be there.

If nothing else, I hope you put a hand up now and then and brush it against that spiritual cord as a reminder that it's still there. As a reminder that you are not alone. And I hope that act renews your soul with strength.

That cord is Jesus. That cord is the Spirit. That cord is hope. That cord is unbroken, even if you are not.

16

BLUE HUES

Jesus in the Dawning of Our Souls

It's—impossibly—Advent again, which means it is also almost the winter solstice, which also means it's been nearly one year since Jenn died. Our Christmas tree is up once again. I've added to my Christmas village and Christmas décor. I have baked and shopped and prepped for the holiday. I've done the Christmas things you are supposed to do. All the while, I am sitting with this devastating miracle: An entire year has occurred. This year has certainly happened *to me* more than I've moved *through it*, but nonetheless, a year has passed. I have survived a year.

This is the way of it. Whatever your loss looks like, whatever shape the dark night takes, every minute, day, month, year that passes is not just about existing—it is about becoming. You have survived another space of time you did not think you could get through. You have built new resilience muscles. You have grown in capacity. And to become braver is a Jupiter-sized accomplishment.

A couple of days ago, I pulled a book off my bookshelf, Dr. Alicia Britt Chole's *The Night Is Normal*, to loan to a friend. I noticed a piece of paper sticking out from one of the pages. To my utter shock, the paper was a little note from Jenn. I must have used it as a bookmark but forgotten somehow. On it, she'd written, "To: Aubrica Rockstar," her nickname for me, with a little heart over the "i." And where she normally would have written, "From: Jennifer McBooty," my nickname for her, she'd changed it to "From: Jennifer Mc*Beauty*."

She'd underlined the *beaut* and added a smiley face. I laughed aloud. Then I sighed aloud at the sad awe of discovering another found thing. So much of my grief is spent mourning *this*—all the little, silly nothings like nicknames and notes that make a friendship. So many of them are forgotten, or will be soon, if not for surprising reminders now and then.

I've heard that at some point the memories of loss won't always bring intense sorrow and despair, that eventually remembrances can bring joy and thankfulness, though this process takes time. Let's you and me keep reminding ourselves of that. There is no correct timeline to transform our sadness into joy, our dark nights into dawn.

Because healing isn't always that, is it? Joy *instead of* sadness, hope *in place of* despair. It's so often holding both at once, watching for down payments of hope now while also clinging to God's promise of an eschaton, a future when suffering and sadness will be no more (Revelation 21:4). As we wait for that day, healing from loss is less like an arrival—a runner crashing dramatically through a finish line's ribbon—and more like a gradual dawn. Healing in grief is similar to what photographers call the morning blue hour, that half hour or so just before the sun rises, before the first golden light of the morning appears, when the sky and landscape are saturated in soft blues.

Healing in the dark night is not like light busting through or the sun shining brashly. Healing is a subtle, slow, gradient hue of blue.

On the morning of Jenn's one-year, I receive a text from Justin: "The house will be empty today. Come see her if you need to."

So currently I am sitting on Jenn's bedroom floor in front of her urn.

Justin, after almost a year, made a decision, did the next right thing, and purchased a beautiful urn. It's emerald green with bluish undertones and artistic golden grooves. It looks a bit like camouflage. It also has butterflies on it—one for Jenn and for Justin and for each of their children. Jenn's mom has been angry at how breast cancer stole so much of Jenn's physical beauty, her womanliness. Jenn grieved that as well. So this urn, while difficult to look at because of what it is, because of what it holds, is a beautiful resting place at last.

I've heard people say they don't need a grave to visit or an urn to look at. They know their person's soul is in heaven, and that's enough. But I have needed a physical location, a place to meet Jenn. I have wanted that ordinary location, a place to have secret chats with my BFF. And maybe it's weird, but I love sitting here on my best friend's bedroom floor chatting *at* her urn, as if she will answer back. Sometimes I imagine she does. When you lose the person who would have been your support person in grief, it just makes sense to have out-loud imaginary conversations.

In this bedroom, her clothes are here, the little jewelry box I gave her is here. Her journals are here. Her ashes are here. But she is not here.

One day I'll see her again, my faith tells me, on a distant shore. For now, I am going to hug Jenn's urn to my chest. Then get up to leave her room. I will sit on her stairs and sob for a bit. Then eventually I will take a deep breath, stand up, and walk out Jenn's front door into the day's light and December's newest snowfall.

When I walk out the front door, I see, to my utter shock, one of my friends standing outside Jenn's door. She has a small cake in her hand, and I can tell she's alarmed at the sight of me, because she sputters, "Oh! Oh! Oh! I didn't expect to see you. I am so sorry. Ignore me. I was dropping off this cake for Justin and the boys and was going to your house next, but I saw your car in the driveway." She gestures to a box of gourmet caramel popcorn placed on the trunk of my car.

She's flustered because she didn't want to be seen, wanted to drop off the surprise and then dart before being noticed. But I know something she doesn't: This is God saying, *I see you, Aubrey. You are not alone.* All those prayers of *God, where are you?* are answered in this surprising exchange. *This is where I am, Aubrey. Right here. With you. I have been and will be.*

My friend, embarrassed, keeps talking. "Just ignore me. Act like I am not here." Instead, I hug her and she holds me while I shake and sob some more.

Over the course of the day, after I return home, more and more friends stop by my house. They drop off flowers, coffee-shop gift cards, candy, and more. A friend, a piano teacher, sends me a private video of Jenn's son's piano recital. He stumbles through "We Wish You a Merry Christmas," and I sob because Jenn would have been so proud. And I chuckle because she would have been annoyed that he didn't practice more. And I think, *God, thank you for the beautiful collaboration of people who have carried that precious family this year.*

What we find in the dark is a support system, shattered people like you and me who fasten each other to the ground when we feel like we are evaporating. Who mend each other after all the breaking.

☽

A few days after the anniversary of Jenn's passing, in church we sing "Because He Lives," and for the first time in over a year, I sing to Jesus and mean it.

Our worship pastor, Aaron, often reminds our church family that at times we sing worship songs as aspiration. For a long time now, I've attended church services and tried to sing, but mostly I've been posturing or faking it 'til I make it. Sometimes I slink out to cry privately. Other times I want to make a rude hand gesture at Aaron—especially the Sunday he sang, "It Is Well," Jenn's funeral song.

But today is different. Today I find myself able to open my mouth and my heart, to raise my hands and declare,

> Because he lives, I can face tomorrow.
> Because he lives, all fear is gone.[1]

I have lamented that my spiritual formation didn't prepare me for the dark night, but as I sing "Because He Lives," I realize that's not entirely true. Jesus' own crucifixion, Jesus' own dark night of shame and suffering, has formed me, shaped me, saved me.

God sent his Son. They called him Jesus. He lived. He suffered. He died to take away our sins. He befriended the isolated, the grieving, and the afflicted. He sat cross-legged with the downtrodden and the dark-nighted. He heard their stories. He asked them pointed questions. He drew near to the lonely, the confused, the doubting, the ones with hearts so heavy they could not rise from their mats, the ones who had lost everything, the ones who were afraid to dream again, the ones just trying to find a new way forward. And in his own, ultimate dark night on the cross, the Savior screamed to the Father, *God, where are you?*

At the hour of greatest silence, in his own dark night, when God's presence only seemed like absence, Jesus, who is one with the Father, was never, never, never, never abandoned, not truly. And if true for Jesus, then by faith—even faith as modest and brittle as a breadcrumb, even faith that feels as far away as the bunny on the moon—this is also true for us. For you. For me. Even though, in the dark night, we may feel like God's presence disappears, it is only our concepts and our misconceptions about God's presence that do.[2] And that sensation of withdrawal makes possible a new, paradoxical realization: Jesus is *always with us.*

The apostle Paul once announced to the Corinthian church that we always carry the death of Jesus in our bodies so that the life of Jesus might be revealed in our bodies too (2 Corinthians 4:10). When we have loved someone and lost them, we carry them around with us. We gather them up in the folds of our skin. We hold them in our laps. Of course, this is true in the profoundest sense through the Spirit with Jesus; that's what Paul meant. Jesus, our lion in the night, our lamppost, says we are not alone. No one is alone in the night, not really. Not forever.

"We live by faith, not by sight" (2 Corinthians 5:7). This is also something the apostle Paul wrote to the Corinthians, after a strenuous season of difficulty and conflict. Paul was pointing them to the Cross of Jesus—a suffering love. He was reminding them to hold on to their hope in Jesus even when they felt far away from God. He was reminding them that it's in weakness, failure, humility, loss, sleeplessness and hunger, hardship and distress, trouble—it's in the dark night—where and how we truly know Jesus. This is how we prove God.

What we find in the dark is that we have never been alone.

Who we find in the dark is Jesus.

•

There have been new losses since Jenn died—job changes, relationships ended. I am still in the thick of grief. A colleague gave me some balloons recently, and I ran away crying because the gesture reminded me so much of Jenn I could hardly breathe.

Over a year ago, which feels like a lifetime ago now, I wrote about going to the doctor to talk about Jenn dying and the fact that life felt generally difficult. Back then, I was trying desperately to grasp the tail of what might be happening as the dark night descended. I was attempting to let go and surrender to whatever God was doing in the coming night. I was encouraging us both—you and me—to stay open and curious in these obscure seasons where we don't know what God is up to.

Frankly, I might know less now than I knew then, but somehow, I am sure of this: The strange season of God's obscurity is not a distraction from our faith. It *is* our faith journey, guiding us along the dark path to one end: Jesus. Jesus in the midnights, the bluest hours, and the golden dawning of our souls.

Dr. Gerald G. May writes that in our dark nights, "union with God is neither acquired nor received; it is *realized*, and in that sense it is something that can be yearned for, sought after, and—with God's grace—found."[3]

And that makes me think of you. I wonder where your losses have left you. I wonder if you are okay. I wonder where you are in the night. I wonder if you have found God's grace, if you have re-realized your union with God. I wonder if you are stronger than you were before. From twilight to midnight to the bluest hour, where are you? And where is God in it for you?

In my own dark night of the soul, God has ripped to shreds several notions of who I falsely assumed him to be while somehow expanding my heart and capacity. And I also wonder if that's been true for you. That tends to happen in dark nights. Jerry Sittser, who writes profoundly on loss, having known so much of it himself, describes something similar:

> My despondent mood casts a shadow over everything, even over my faith. On those occasions I find it hard to believe anything at all.
>
> But then I gain perspective. I remind myself that suffering is not unique to us; it is the destiny of humanity. If this world were the only one there is, then suffering has the final say, and all of us are a sorry lot. But generations of faithful Christians have gone before and will come after, and they have believed or will believe what I believe in the depths of my soul. Jesus is at the center of it all. He defeated sin and death through his crucifixion and resurrection. Then light gradually dawns once again in my heart, and hope returns. I find reason and courage

> to keep going and to continue believing. Once again my soul increases its capacity for hope as well as for sadness. I end up believing with greater depth and joy than I had before, even in my sorrow.[4]

I think what Sittser means is that in grief we become the lost thing that is also found: another paradox of the dark night.

☾

When I began this journey with you, I believed, and still believe to some degree, that light is always just on the other side of the moon. That what defines the dark isn't light's absence but its hiddenness. But now I believe something else as well: Our hope in the dark night isn't that daylight returns. Sometimes it stays dark for a long time. Sometimes we don't know if day will ever come again. But in the dark, there's community and friendship. There's Jesus. There's the Spirit. There's God, mysteriously, confoundingly, in it all.

What we find in the dark, if we choose to look though it's hard to see, is love.

REFLECTIONS AND PRACTICES

Part One | NIGHTFALL

1 | Enter the Dark

1. Reflect on this quote: "Someone once said that grief occurs anytime you wish something was more, better, or different. So, in its most basic and ubiquitous form, grief happens when life is not turning out how you expected. Grief isn't limited to loss, or even death." How would you define *grief*? When have you experienced it?

2. *The dark night of the soul* is not a phrase in the Bible, but it's been a spiritual experience of followers of God throughout history. What, if anything, have you been taught or learned about the dark night of the soul or seasons like it? How do you think the church can better normalize this experience for Christians? Why do we tend to struggle with the concept of the dark night of the soul?

3. Have you been in a dark night of the soul? What was/is that like for you? What helped you or is currently helping you hang on?

4. If you were to imagine Jesus with you in the dark, is there a certain image of Jesus or truth about the character of God that is particularly helpful or meaningful to you right now? What is it, and why?

5. Spend some time considering what the dark night of the soul is (see appendix A). What might God be inviting you into?

6. Part of the dark night's work is helping us identify and then release us from our attachments (idols, addictions, habits, etc.). For you it might be striving or overachievement. It might be compulsive shopping or bingeing behaviors. It might even be the need to people please or be codependent. When God shines a light on these things, it is ultimately to set us free, to help us worship him alone, and to move us toward our own souls' lightness and freedom. Take some time to ask the Spirit to help you identify any false attachments. What would freedom look like? Feel like?

2 | Twilight on the Horizon

1. Have you wrestled through a season when you thought life would go one way but it went in an entirely different direction? What was that like for you? What, if anything, have you learned through it?

2. This chapter poses these questions: "On a scale of *I-am-not-where-I-thought-I'd-be-by-now* to *I-am-so-lost-I-can-barely-breathe*, where do you find yourself? What have you lost?

What disruption are you facing?" How would you answer today?

3. Do you have spaces in your life, even in your pain, for delight and fun? How can you cultivate more room for those? And why would they be important or helpful?

4. Do you tend to "ignore the twilight" or face it? What would it look like for you to keep yourself open to what the dark night of the soul might have to teach you, what God might want to do in it?

5. How do you cling to, wrestle for, or look for hope in dark seasons? What helps you? What gives you strength?

3 | The Obscurity of Dusk

1. Have you walked though a season of God's obscurity? What was/is that like for you? How have you seen God at work, even in seeming divine absence?

2. What habits of faith or spiritual practices help you cling to God in darkness?

3. In a journal or in the back of this book (see appendix B for a chart and instructions), use two columns to pay attention to where God is present in the darkness: "Breadcrumbs of Hope" (signs of God's goodness, no matter how small) and "What does this reveal about God's character?" Don't judge yourself or overthink this exercise. Allow it to encourage your faith in the dark.

4 | The Dimly Lit Path

1. Reflect on this proverb: "Hope deferred makes the heart sick" (Proverbs 13:12). What do you think that means? If hope deferred makes the heart sick, what heals the heart?
2. This chapter wrestles with questions like these: "[Loss and] disappointments won't end. What do we do with them? And what about our unwelcome anger, sadness, and grief? Where do we take those when God feels elusive? When our hearts are sick and hope feels gone and God seems far, how do we not just give up searching for him? Why should we even bother?" How would you answer these questions?
3. What do you think Jesus meant when he told us to pray with "shameless audacity" (Luke 11:8)?
4. How does friendship with God allow you to make audacious requests of God?
5. What are you asking of God right now?

5 | Nighttime Losses

1. Have you ever lost anything that was important to you? What was it, and what was that loss like for you?
2. What does it mean to you to know that God loves lost things and lost people?
3. When we lose someone or something special, that person or item is never truly replaced, but sometimes God brings new gifts into our lives—new relationships, new adventures that

wouldn't be there if we were still clinging to the past. Have you experienced that? When and how?

4. Wrestle with this statement: "J. R. R. Tolkien once implied that because of Jesus everything sad will one day come untrue, and it will somehow be greater for having been broken. I like to believe, similarly, that everything lost will be found again in Jesus. Or, as Frederick Buechner once said, 'What's lost is nothing to what's found, and all the death that ever was, set next to life, would scarcely fill a cup.'" What do you think Tolkien and Buechner meant?

Part Two | MIDNIGHT

If you're in fresh grief or a midnight of the soul, the last thing you need is another series of questions or homework to add to your to-do list. In this section, I am inviting you to practice some spiritual habits for midnight: rest, slowing down, silence, breath prayers, and intimacy with God. Do these now. Do these later. It doesn't matter, just as long as you are gentle with yourself in the doing. See appendix C for a guide.

Part Three | NIGHT-LIGHTS

12 | Floating Lanterns

1. Reflect on this quote: "Whether you've lost someone to death or lost something that meant something to you, the choice to start over or to step forward or to be brave is a bit like voluntarily lying down on a surgical table without

knowing if you are under the care of a skilled surgeon or a hack. Hopefully the heart transplant goes okay, but you don't really know if it will. It's all a life-threatening risk." What risks and fears are keeping you from stepping forward in your grief?

2. What would it look like for you to "do it scared"—to step into life or take a risk or start something new even when you are afraid?

3. What about time moving forward makes it hard as you are grieving? Why do you think that experience is so difficult for most grievers?

4. Do you currently find it challenging or interesting or exciting to open your heart to new people and new adventures? Maybe a bit of all three? And in what ways? What, if anything, are you sensing God inviting you to try?

13 | Northern Lights

1. Take some time to consider some of the ways God has shown up for you in the middle of your grief or dark nights. If you haven't done so, begin to make a list of those ways.

2. What gifts are you discovering, or lessons are you learning, in your midnight or current season that you might not be able to find at other times? What is God uniquely revealing to you here, in this dark place? If you were to create a list of found things, what might be on it?

3. If making a list is a struggle for you, why? What might God's Spirit be inviting you into now? How might a list of the ways God is showing up be helpful for your faith?

4. In what ways are you beginning to sense your soul wanting to come back to life or live more fully again after loss?

14 | Illuminations

1. Reflect on this quote: "So many of us feel like this—a little unsure of our voice, our place, our opinions. We doubt ourselves. We second-guess our value. We feel like imposters. We say yes when we want to say no. We were socialized not to let anyone down, or not to trust ourselves, or to say yes so people will like us, approve of us." Has this been true in your life? If so, how? When does your own imposter syndrome or people-pleasing creep in?

2. How does grief allow you to be more certain and confident about your yeses and nos?

3. Think about your own yeses and nos. What's the experience of saying them like for you? Are you someone who struggles with people-pleasing, with saying no when you want to? What has the journey of finding and using your voice and your agency been like for you?

4. Have you ever felt like you existed as an apology? What was that like? If you've experienced any freedom from that kind of thinking or another limiting belief, what is it like to take up more space?

15 | Satellites and Starlight

1. Read Psalm 40 aloud slowly. As you hear the words, note anything that stands out, any questions you have, anything that strikes you. Assume that *that* is God's Spirit speaking to you, showing you something.

2. Have you struggled in your grief to read the Bible or listen to worship music or pray or attend church events? What's that been like? What would it be like to take a tiny step toward some of those experiences of connection with God again? If this has not been a struggle for you, how might you gently encourage someone else who is wrestling in this way?

3. What is bringing you hope right now? What are you believing about God and the dark night right now? In what ways have you been pleasantly surprised by the dark night of the soul? What unexpected lessons have you learned about yourself, God, or spiritual seasons like this? In what ways are you still struggling? In what ways are you finding some healing and new hope?

16 | Blue Hues

1. What has staying faithful to God and to yourself in your dark night looked like? How might this be different from your faithfulness in other seasons?

2. If you were to describe the dark night of the soul to a friend who is walking through one, explaining what you have found God doing in it, what might you say?

3. How are you different now than you were a year or so ago? How has your relationship with God changed? How have you grown or deepened?
4. Evaluate your current dark night. Are you in a midnight? Are you sensing any movement toward the blue hue of morning? How does this movement or lack thereof make you feel?
5. Consider Jesus in his own dark night of the soul. Consider Paul and the early church in theirs. What do we learn from Jesus? What do we learn from the people of faith before us?
6. If you could ask God to do anything in your dark night or your grief right now, what would it be? Spend some time crafting and praying a raw, honest prayer.

APPENDIX A

WHAT IS THE DARK NIGHT OF THE SOUL?

Where does the phrase *dark night of the soul* come from?	Coined by St. John of the Cross and St. Teresa of Ávila in the late 1500s and early 1600s, Spain. This is a way to describe an experience of God's felt absence.
What is the dark night of the soul?	An experience (of any length of time and often repeated any number of times) for the follower of Jesus where God intentionally removes the sense of his presence. Why? So the Spirit can empty us of our distorted images of God and our false identities and also release us from our unhealthy attachments.
What *isn't* the dark night?	Depression, grief, sin, trauma, spiritual attack, spiritual immaturity, or "going backward" (though there might be overlap with any of these in the dark night, which can make it confusing).

What is God doing in the dark night?	Removing your ideas of his presence but not his actual presence. Releasing you from attachments and anxieties. Reminding you of your true identity. Requesting you join him in a "night" faith—a faith that endures through the unknown, the mysterious, and the painful.
What can you do in the dark night?	Cry out to God in lament. Create—not for production but to express your emotions. Be in safe, healthy Christian community. Commune with God as best you can. Recall God's character and faithfulness over the course of your entire life and as witnessed to in the Scriptures. Relinquish any illusion of control; surrender to whatever God is up to. Take up the "Spiritual Practices for Midnight" (see appendix C) while waiting patiently.

APPENDIX B

BREADCRUMBS OF HOPE

Don't judge yourself or overthink this exercise. Simply jot down some of the ways God meets you this week. Maybe it's through an unexpected provision or gift. Maybe God gives you some time to yourself for renewal or some meaningful moments with friends. Perhaps you read or hear a word from someone wise or God speaks to you in another way. Maybe you find something you thought was lost. Write these "breadcrumbs" down throughout the week(s) in the first column. Then in the second column write what these reveal about God's character. For example, *God is a provider. God lavishes me with unexpected encouragement. God is creative and good. God is working behind the scenes, even when I can't see it.* Spend some time thanking God for big and small provisions of hope and abundance, even in the dark night. Praise him for his faithfulness, even when the days are painful.

Breadcrumb of Hope	**What does this reveal about God's character?**

APPENDIX C

SPIRITUAL PRACTICES FOR MIDNIGHT

Rest

In our dark nights of the soul, we are being invited to release *hustle* and instead pick up *rest, trust, surrender.*[1] At times this can be difficult to do, especially if we are among those whose internal engine is always on so that we can avoid feeling our pain. We might be afraid to rest because we know that the moment we stop, we will have to face our heartache. But in not resting, we make ourselves bone-weary and burned out in our bodies and souls. That's not what God wants for us.

A regular spiritual practice of rest is beneficial physically, emotionally, and spiritually—especially in loss and spiritual dark nights—because it allows us to honor our limits and remember the things we used to find delight and joy in. Those can be difficult to remember when pain and grief demand so much of our capacity.

Rest doesn't have to look like ceasing; it might be a nap, but it can also be taking a long walk or doing something that's soul filling and enjoyable. Maybe rest looks like taking yourself to the movies, going on a hike with a friend, painting, watching your favorite movie, or reading some poetry. Consider a list of things that would be restful for you, then schedule an hour or a day or an entire weekend of rest for them.

Note what this does in your soul and your body and how God meets you when you are rested. What are you better able to face? What are you better able to release? How does your grief respond to rest?

Rest is ultimately a counterliturgy to the pressure of attachments and anxieties. Rest says you are a human being, not a human doing. You have needs, and you are not enslaved to that which demands restlessness.

Slowing Down

Slowing down is just what it sounds like: less hurry, more margin, greater availability to divine interruption. Slowing down might feel impossible to you; it might even seem like it will add more stress to your day. But the point of slowing down is to be more responsive to God's invitation to rest, to breathe, to be present to relationships. Hurried people are anxious people, often avoiding the feelings of loss underneath. Slowing down invites us to pay attention to our soul's needs and to God's desires for us.

Spend some time practicing slowness. Here are some examples:

- Read slowly.
- Drive in the slow lane.
- Choose the longest checkout line at the store.
- Schedule extra time between your meetings.
- Slowly read a psalm.

- Set an alarm for every few hours to pause from whatever you are doing and pray the Jesus Prayer: "Lord Jesus Christ, Son of God, have mercy on me, a sinner."
- Breathe deeply before moving on to the next task on your list.

Remember the old adage at the pool: "Walk, don't run." That's the theme of slowing down.

Later, reflect on your day through the lens of slowness. What was it like for you to move slower? When did you find it difficult to slow down? When were you most able to move slowly? What lies have you believed about a fast pace? How might slowness help you in your grief and dark night?

Silence

Silence is another spiritual practice where you don't have to do much; this is simply a time to try to tune your attention away from the cacophony of distractions and "noise" in life—even your own voice and opinions, along with the disparate voices of others. In grief and dark nights, there are people who will accost you with hollow advice or who will choose not to say anything at all (when you desperately want them to ask you about your loss). All those voices, opinions, and unspoken words are difficult to receive in grief. So we practice silence to hear the one still, small voice of God.

Sometimes silence simply looks like monotasking. Turn off the music or the podcast or the audiobook for a time while you are driving or studying or doing dishes or cooking. Just do one thing at a time. Make breakfast before you start the laundry. Finish one book at a time. Don't multitask.

But most often silence looks like a time set aside for intentionally avoiding distraction, getting quiet, becoming present, and being in the moment.

Place yourself somewhere quiet. (If you're a mama or daddy with littles, moments in the car or even a five-minute shower are good for this.) Turn off any background noise. Silence your phone (better yet—put that phone far away from you). Inhale and exhale, asking God to meet you in the quiet. Then do just that: Spend some time being quiet. That's about it.

You might begin by lighting a candle and meditating silently on a favorite Bible verse or by asking God's Spirit to move toward you with love; then spend some silent time listening, being present, and so on. Practices like silence are more passive than active, allowing you to still yourself to be more attentive to God's activity in your life.

Don't worry if your mind runs off or if you get distracted; that's part of the process. In fact, wherever your mind is running to—that just might be an invitation from God, something God wants you to focus on, something the Spirit wants to connect with you about. Don't critique or judge yourself. Silence is difficult for most people. Some people have found it helpful to imagine a gently flowing river as they practice silence. When they get distracted, they simply "place" that thought into the river like a leaf, allowing the water to carry it away. In other cases, they choose to follow the distracted thought wherever the Spirit is leading.

The goal is not to "win" at silence or to zone out. The goal is to be present with God, without distractions, so you can hear that still, small voice of the Spirit speaking into your heartache and longings. Later, reflect on what silence was like for you. What was difficult about it? Could you imagine doing an entire day of silence?

Breath Prayers

Breath prayers are a practice that most people believe started with the ancient desert fathers and mothers. The idea is that praying becomes as natural as breathing. Today, breath prayer is often used as a way to de-stress, refocus, and perhaps reflect on a passage of Scripture. Breathing is an instinctual act, but many of us neglect our breathing as a byproduct of ignoring the needs of our bodies—and even more so when grief has undermined our everyday living. Throughout the Scriptures, there are brief lines and verses that can be read in a rhythm of inhale-exhale, and those lines can function as a counterliturgy to the hurried, anxious life rhythm that grief can foist on us.

To begin practicing a breath prayer, choose a passage of Scripture you connect with and simply meditate on it, repeating the words and phrases as you breathe in and out. An example to start with is a breath prayer from Psalm 46:10. Inhale slowly to the words *Be still.* Pause and consider God's presence. Then exhale to the words *and know.*[2]

The point is to breathe in God's Word slowly and deeply and exhale your anxieties.

Intimacy with God

I am mentioning this as a broad category under "Spiritual Practices for Midnight" because increasingly I sense, at least in some parts of Christian culture, a legalistic push to practice spiritual habits in the "right" way at the "right" time. But because every person's grief and individual context is unique, not everyone has the life luxury or the emotional wherewithal for a weekend, a day, or even an hour for things like rest, silence, or stillness. The moment spiritual practices become legalistic or performative instead of being a means of grace, they've lost their purpose.

Ultimately (as I hope you've picked up while reading this book) I want you to do whatever you need to do to stay connected to God while giving yourself a whole lot of grace for all the things you can't do. For me, staying connected to Jesus happenened by asking God my raw questions, researching the dark night of the soul, writing, meeting with my spiritual director, looking for glimpses of hope, being in community, and reading the Psalms bit by bit (as you read in chapter 15).

For you, intimacy with Jesus might look like listening to thoughtful worship music, meditating on Scripture, creating art, prayer journaling, or serving in community. The point is, I hesitate to prescribe *a specific way* of taking up spiritual practices for your midnight. But I can assure you that any gentle, graceful habit of intimacy with God, any movement toward God, however small, will be a lifeline in your pain. God will meet you there.

Acknowledgments

How to thank the people who have carried you during one of the most treacherous seasons you've walked? I guess you start by starting.

To Kevin and the boys: You are my shining lights in the dark night. I love you. I like you. I adore you.

To the Squad: I dedicated this book to you as a way to mark this strange, sad, sacred moment in time that we have shared as foxhole sisters. I am so sorry we have borne it but so grateful we weren't alone.

To Carrie and Julie M.: I lost a friend. You lost a friend, sista love, daughter, and your person all in one. You are brave and gorgi, and you both have my heart.

To Justin and the boys: You keep showing up, and you are doing such a good job. She is proud of you.

To the entire NavPress team: Thank you for loving these words into existence. To my editor, Caitlyn Carlson: You kept reminding me to be a whole person rather than a Horcrux as I wrote. And in so doing, you allowed my grief to take up as much space as it needed while helping me find a path through it. Thank you for tending to my heart as you tended to this manuscript.

To Ingrid Beck, my lovely agent, who is a dollface and amazing.

To the Propel Women coaches: You are my sisters and my people. I love you and this ministry so much.

To the Nothing Is Wasted ministry team: I'm so grateful for you, for our partnership in the gospel, and for the work we do.

To my Renewal Church family: You've borne this loss and so many others during the past few years. I know it has been heavy to carry. You are the most beautiful, beloved community in all the universe.

To my family and to so many of my dear, dear friends: There are too many of you to name (but you know who you are), and that is an absolute miracle for which I praise God. You show up. You stay faithful. You exchange a lot of long-winded voice messages with me throughout the day. I am so grateful for you.

And I would be remiss not to thank two Catholic mystics, St. John of the Cross and St. Teresa of Ávila. Though our ecclesiological traditions—not to mention hundreds and hundreds of years—seek to separate us, these two became my unanticipated grief companions. Their passion for prayer and the church as well as their commitment to find God in the dark ministered to my soul. (There is perhaps a word here for us all about the ripple effect of our fidelity to God: We have no idea how God might use our faithfulness in dark nights to minister to future generations.)

And, of course, to you, beloved reader: I write for your pain. I pray for you as you hurt. I keep going for you. May you know you are not alone because Jesus is here, under the moon and the stars, or wherever else you find yourself.

Notes

AN OPENING CONFESSION | THIS IS NOT WHAT I PLANNED FOR

1. Barbara Brown Taylor, *Learning to Walk in the Dark* (New York: HarperOne, 2015), 55.
2. David C. Downing, foreword to Jerry Root, *Splendour in the Dark: C. S. Lewis's* Dymer *in His Life and Work* (Downers Grove, IL: InterVarsity Press, 2020), 5.

1 | ENTER THE DARK

1. Barbara Brown Taylor, *Learning to Walk in the Dark* (New York: HarperOne, 2015), 135.
2. Gerald G. May, *The Dark Night of the Soul: A Psychiatrist Explores the Connection Between Darkness and Spiritual Growth* (San Francisco: HarperSanFrancisco, 2004), 20–21.
3. John Mark Comer, "The Dark Night of the Soul Pt. 2: Naming Your Stage of Apprenticeship," sermon, Bridgetown Church, Portland, Oregon, June 9, 2019, MP3 audio file, 52:58, https://bridgetown.church/teachings/naming-your-stage-of-apprenticeship/the-dark-night-of-the-soul-pt-2.
4. May, *Dark Night of the Soul*, 7.

3 | THE OBSCURITY OF DUSK

1. St. John of the Cross, *Ascent of Mount Carmel*, trans. P. Silverio de Santa Teresa, ed. E. Allison Peers (Westminster, MD: Newman Bookshop, 1945; repr., Eastford, CT: Martino Fine Books, 2016), 70.
2. Beth Moore, "Episode 260—Discovering God's Faithfulness in Our Knotted-Up Lives with Beth Moore," interview by Aubrey Sampson and Davey Blackburn, *Nothing Is Wasted*, podcast, February 23, 2024, https://www.nothingiswasted.com/podcast1/episode-260.

3. Walter Brueggemann, *Living Toward a Vision: Biblical Reflections on Shalom* (Philadelphia: United Church Press, 1976), 51.

5 | NIGHTTIME LOSSES

1. This idea is from J. R. R. Tolkien's *The Return of the King* (New York: Ballantine Books, 1985), 283, but was used in this way by Tim Keller (@TimothyKeller), Facebook, January 18, 2016, https://www.facebook.com/TimKellerNYC/posts/1075542919152260.
2. Frederick Buechner, *Godric* (San Francisco: HarperSanFrancisco, 1983), 96.

6 | THE LONGEST HOURS

1. Joan Didion, "After Death," *New York Times*, September 25, 2005, https://www.nytimes.com/2005/09/25/magazine/after-life.html. "Our days were filled with the sound of each other's voices."
2. Margaret Edson, *Wit: A Play* (New York: Farrar, Straus and Giroux, 1999), 15.
3. Douglas Kaine McKelvey, "An Exhortation: Making Space to Speak of Dying," in *Every Moment Holy*, volume 2, *Death, Grief, and Hope* (Nashville: Rabbit Room Press, 2021), page 27. "The veil is thinner than we know. / And death is thinner still."
4. Kathy Khang and Matt Mikalatos, *Loving Disagreement: Fighting for Community Through the Fruit of the Spirit* (Colorado Springs: NavPress, 2023), 140.
5. Inspired by a line from Nichole Nordeman, "Small Enough," track 5, *This Mystery*, Sparrow Records, 2000: "Oh, great God / Be small enough to hear me now."

7 | TOSSING AND TURNING

1. "Strong's H30—*'ĕlōhîm*," Blue Letter Bible, accessed September 12, 2024, https://www.blueletterbible.org/lexicon/h430/kjv/wlc/0-1.
2. E. B. White, *Charlotte's Web*, reprint ed. (New York: HarperCollins, 2012), 164.

8 | SHIFTING SHADOWS

1. Gerald G. May, *The Dark Night of the Soul: A Psychiatrist Explores the Connection Between Darkness and Spiritual Growth* (San Francisco: HarperSanFrancisco, 2004), 80–81.
2. May, *Dark Night of the Soul*, 67–68.
3. John O'Donohue, "Entering Death," in *To Bless the Space Between Us: A Book of Blessings* (New York: Doubleday, 2008), 179. "May your going be sheltered / And your welcome assured."

NOTES

9 | HOLDING ON IN THE DARK

1. Grace P. Cho, "Release in Me a Song of Lament," in *Voices of Lament: Reflections on Brokenness and Hope in a World Longing for Justice*, ed. Natasha Sistrunk Robinson (Grand Rapids: Revell, 2022), 213. The poem is a cry inextricably bound up with the loss of her halmoni, her grandmother.
2. Viktor E. Frankl, *Man's Search for Meaning*, trans. Ilse Lasch (Boston: Beacon Press, 2006), 113, 138.
3. Fleming Rutledge, *Means of Grace: A Year of Weekly Devotions*, ed. Laura Bardolph Hubers (Grand Rapids: Eerdmans, 2021), 5.

10 | A STRANGE NEW ORBIT

1. Edna St. Vincent Millay, "Millay to Llewelyn Powys, April 20, 1931," in *Into the World's Great Heart: Selected Letters of Edna St. Vincent Millay*, ed. Timothy F. Jackson (New Haven, CT: Yale University Press, 2023), 255–56.
2. *WandaVision*, season one, episode eight, "Previously On," created by Jac Schaeffer, directed by Matt Shakman, aired February 26, 2021, on Disney+.

11 | THE STILL OF THE NIGHT

1. This analogy can be found many places online, including at Sandra Silva, PsychCentral, updated October 13, 2021, https://psychcentral.com/blog/coping-with-grief-ball-and-box-analogy.
2. This section is informed by St. John of the Cross, *Ascent of Mount Carmel*, trans. P. Silverio de Santa Teresa, ed. E. Allison Peers (Westminster, MD: Newman Bookshop, 1945; repr., Eastford, CT: Martino Fine Books, 2016), 84–86.

12 | FLOATING LANTERNS

1. Jerry Sittser, *A Grace Disguised: How the Soul Grows Through Loss*, rev. ed. (Grand Rapids: Zondervan, 2021), 172. Here Sittser writes, "Choosing to withdraw from people and to protect the self diminishes the soul; choosing to love even more deeply than before ensures that we will suffer again, for the choice to love requires the courage to grieve."

13 | NORTHERN LIGHTS

1. Of course, Galentine's Day is a holiday made famous by Leslie Knope on *Parks and Recreation*, season 2, episode 16, directed by Ken Kwapis, written by Greg Daniels, Michael Schur, and Katie Dippold, featuring Amy Poehler as Leslie Knope, aired February 11, 2010, on NBC.

14 | ILLUMINATIONS

1. *Say Anything* (Los Angeles: Gracie Films and Twentieth Century Fox, 1989).

15 | SATELLITES AND STARLIGHT

1. "Strong's H6960—*qāvâ*," Blue Letter Bible, accessed July 10, 2024, https://www.blueletterbible.org/lexicon/h6960/kjv/wlc/0-1; and "Strong's H8615—*tiqvâ*," Blue Letter Bible, accessed July 10, 2024, https://www.blueletterbible.org/lexicon/h8615/kjv/wlc/0-1.
2. See appendix C for a description of some midnight practices for your own formation.

16 | BLUE HUES

1. "Because He Lives," written by Gloria Gaither and Bill Gaither, Capitol CMG/Hanna Street Music, 2018. Originally released in 1971.
2. As Gerald May writes, "As John [of the Cross] makes clear, it is not God who disappears, but only our concepts, images, and sensations *of* God. This relinquishment occurs to rid us of our attachment to these idols and to make possible a realization of the true God, who cannot be grasped by any thought or feeling. At the time though, it seems like abandonment, even betrayal." Gerald G. May, *The Dark Night of the Soul: A Psychiatrist Explores the Connection Between Darkness and Spiritual Growth* (San Francisco: HarperSanFrancisco, 2004), 146–47.
3. May, *Dark Night of the Soul*, 47.
4. Jerry Sittser, *A Grace Disguised: How the Soul Grows Through Loss*, rev. ed. (Grand Rapids: Zondervan, 2021), 169.

APPENDIX C | SPIRITUAL PRACTICES FOR MIDNIGHT

1. For more spiritual practices, see Adele Ahlberg Calhoun's *Spiritual Disciplines Handbook: Practices That Transform Us*, rev. and exp. ed. (Downers Grove, IL: InterVarsity Press, 2015).
2. For additional suggestions, see Bill Gaultiere, "Breath Prayers," Soul Shepherding, accessed September 17, 2024, https://www.soulshepherding.org/breath-prayers.

More from Aubrey Sampson

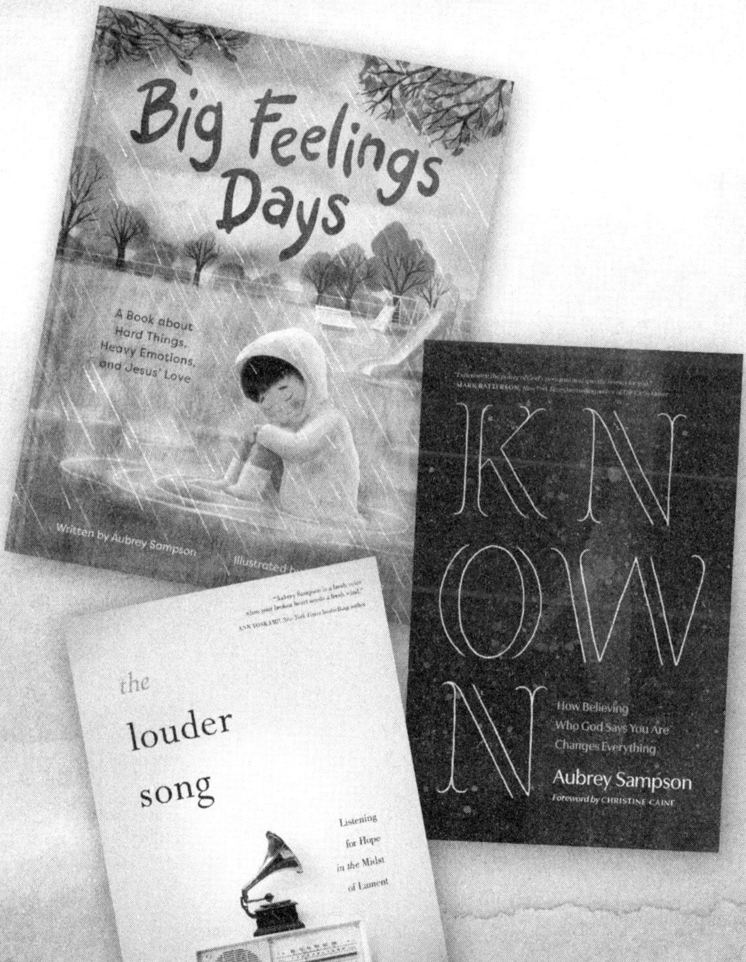

NavPress

CP2026